THE CIRCLE
OF LIFE

THE CIRCLE OF LIFE

Caring *for* Our Loved Ones:
Faith, Family, *and* Balance

LINDA BAUTERS

credo
house publishers

Published in the United States of America by Credo House Publishers, a division
of Credo Communications LLC, Grand Rapids, Michigan
credohousepublishers.com

ISBN: 978-1-62586-206-8

Cover and interior design by Jonathan Lewis
Editing by Donna Huisjen

Printed in the United States of America
First edition

Contents

Minute Meditation by Franciscan Media

August 22, 2014

Today Be Joyful

We know we are not always going to be happy. Sadness, even trag-edy, is going to cross our paths more than once. But if we strive to be joyful on a daily *basis* we seem to develop reserves upon which we can draw.

—from *Be Joyful Daily* by Pope Frances and *Our Call to Duty*

Preface

MY BOOK TOUCHES on life, death, and all that is in between. It deals with the fundamental basis of our faith, our knowing that there is something else beyond our lives here on this earth. Do we live, only to die? This enigma is a tough one. The purpose of this book is not to give expert advice. My hope is that by relaying my experiences through caring for my children, parents, and uncle and working as a Certified Nursing Assistant (CNA), I may help you and provide inspiration. My stories are those shared by many caregivers. Our time on this earth is truly short, and how we spend it is up to us. I have found in progressing through my life that when one chapter or door closes, another one invariably opens.

Our parents brought us here and gave us life. Whether your birth parents, other family members, a foster parent, or an adoptive parent, there was, hopefully, someone who cared for you. They helped us develop into adulthood. Then, as adults, we in our turn help them through the aging and death process. If we have children, there may come a time when they will be hopefully, able and willing to help us.

That becomes the circle of life. I will relay my experiences as a series of stories. I have read many articles and books and have gone for guidance to self-help classes relating to Alzheimer's, dementia, and Parkinson's disease. I have relied on prayers, been inspired over the years by others, especially my spouse, our children, my sisters, their husbands, aunts, uncles, nieces, nephews, and friends. What also has provided inspiration are Minute Meditations by Franciscan Media, which I receive via email.

It is with both sadness and hope that I tell you that both my parents are deceased. The sadness is that I cannot see them, hear their voices, sit at their kitchen table to have coffee and meals together, listen to stories about growing up in quite different times than we are in now, laugh and cry with them. It is with hope that I look forward to being reunited with them one day.

There is no greater love than that between a parent and a child. No matter what the disappointments in your childhood, you are an extension of your parents. There is no absolute right way to raise a child or care for a parent. There is no book that will give all the answers. All the "how tos" are guides that provide tools for us to use as aids. The real compass, though, is what is inside us. The opportunities, roadblocks, failures, limitations, and opportunities are the impetus of our life. What to do in any given situation is never cut and dry. My husband of over thirty years has said, "Always try to do the right thing." The key word is to *try*. We will make mistakes along the way that build us up through the journey of living.

It is difficult to fathom the coping mechanisms when a young child, teen, adult, or older person has a debilitating disease or ailment, whether it is mental or physical. Every day, day in and day out, there is that question of how both they and you (as caregiver) will muddle through. We try to plow through physical and mental limitations. A person who will not get better has to deal with this reality and continue coping for as long as they can. When someone dies, whether they leave this earth quickly or slowly, it is devastating for us. But the journey for their survivors does not end. Time continues to move on. The memories and reminders of those who are gone stay with us throughout our lives. We continue to cling to fond and beautiful life stories, often minimizing or even repressing memories of the hard times.

Our lives are a series of stories. My husband and I have helped and cared for loved ones with attention deficit hyperactivity disorder (ADHD), dementia, Alzheimer's, Parkinson's, heart and skin disease, diabetes, osteoporosis, congestive heart failure (CHF), cancer, and depression, to name a few of the many ailments we have encountered. How does one stay positive?

The body breaks down to its simplest form. As a caregiver, you are often watching the body and mind of the person you are caring for slowly wither away. As this is happening to that person, you as a caregiver feel a replication of the process within yourself. It is not easy for those involved to say and think that each day truly is a blessing. There is that inner struggle within your loved one and yourself to come to peace. How can you feel peaceful when so many painful and unpleasant things are happening with your loved one?

We are still dealing with all this inner turmoil, including the demons we experience within ourselves. It is a process. Emotions both tear us down and build us up. In caring for my parents, other older individuals, and those who have a lifelong debilitating illness, I have seen how their focus tends to be on themselves. Their world gets smaller and smaller. It is natural to become self-absorbed. The center of the universe becomes *you*. Just as with the progression from infant to toddler to child, *time changes things*.

In the words of William Shakespeare in *Twelfth Night*, "O time, thou must untangle this, not I; it is too hard a knot for me to untie." Time can solve some problems. Time is an ointment for broken hearts, a healer of dissolved friendships, a restorer of failed health and lost fortune. Time has the power to dry tears, steady nerves, renew courage, and see through the haze. As time moves on, it changes circumstances. What a powerful and hopeful thought. When you wake up the next day you can take on whatever obstacles come up. As time keeps turning, hope provides the courage to continue.

Life entails a lot of small successes that propel us to do more. It's all about how we handle each day-to-day challenge that combine to make up a lifetime of events. Our life is a story. In caring for loved ones, the common thread is family. Our family, with all its idiosyncrasies, is central to what we have. Everyone has a story to tell. I have struggles and do things the hard way but have learned about life and continue to learn. In rendering all my stories about children, parents, family, and caregiving, I recognize that each person has unique and special qualities that are in each of us.

Introduction

THE CHILDREN WE were blessed with are each a miracle. I had severe endometriosis, necessitating my having major surgery three months before getting married and another surgery three years later. In between all this, I was on numerous medications and had many tests. The ironic thing is that I did not think I wanted any children, as I expressed to my now husband. This almost broke us apart before our getting engaged. He came from a family of ten and wanted ten children. That is a far cry from zero! I was so wrong about want I thought I wanted, what I needed and was ultimately given in my life!

Thank goodness God was looking over me because we have four children. To this day I thank God; Dr. Joan Stryker, my gynecologist; and another surgeon who had expertise in performing surgery for women with endometriosis. He removed as much of the scar tissue as possible, leaving fifteen percent of one ovary and ten percent of the other. Any other surgeon would likely have said I required a hysterectomy. This outcome left only a minimal probability of my getting pregnant but did offer some small chance and a ray of hope that it could happen. It did happen, naturally, three years later. I had two miscarriages between two of my children. I can say now that my best gifts ever are my husband, our children, and our extended family.

My circle of life has come about three quarters of the way around. Where are you in your circle? I have spent a large amount of my time caring for my children, parents, and relatives and functioning as a CNA worker. I am not an expert, famous, or a holy roller. Life takes many unexpected turns. My hope is that I can help you in some way by sharing my stories. We strive for the best, the most, and all that is in between. Life is a journey. I have relied on prayers, my spouse, and reading via the internet, particularly *Minute Meditations* by Franciscan Media. These meditations are brief excerpts that have helped me get through so many days of fear, uncertainty, and challenges. Every day I must work at doing better and being positive.

The past is what shapes us. There are events that happened, good and bad, that affect our future. The bad events can incapacitate us in terms of our ability to function in the present, just as a computer virus can invade and halt its operational functions. The past comes forward to invade the present and, although much of it is "ancient" history, remains deeply entangled within us. Without realizing it, we find ourselves held in a historical trauma that continues, often causing sadness and anger. I know—I am my own worst enemy. Life is a journey.

Minute Meditation by Franciscan Media
Sunday, September 1, 2013

Hope Provides Freedom

Hope provides the freedom to live at peace with ourselves, *others* and God, regardless of what may be going on around us.

—from *Real Women, Real Saints* by Gina Loehr

CHAPTER 1

The Circle of Life: Children and Family

A S A BABY we rely on someone else for everything. Babies are completely dependent on us to do everything for them. At that stage in our little ones' lives, we are sleep deprived, with the baby demanding our full attention morning, noon, and night! In the insanity of all the activities, each stage can seem all-encompassing and overwhelming. This season requires taking care of ourselves physically, mentally, and spiritually. Then we continue through our lives with the goal of keeping our inner balance and being fulfilled. Together this combination lends to our living a grateful and happy life.

As a child, we deal with being accepted by our friends, trying to excel in school, and living up to our parents' expectations. As we grow into adulthood, we may get married, have children, buy a house, and work to maintain all we have and want. Children require a lot of energy to take care of, nurture, and raise to become good Christians. Children are a beautiful gift, and I am grateful to be blessed with them.

It is true, issues grow larger as the child gets older. If you have children, you try to help them become all they are capable of being. Then they continue to grow through adolescence into their teens. Those teen years can be tough for you and your son or daughter. It becomes clear that babies are easy compared to experiencing those teenage years. Through those years I witnessed my children's rebellion with life, finding themselves, fitting in at school, and struggling with living. This can carry over into college years and beyond.

Our children hopefully grow up to become independent, while our parents grow older and feebler and become more dependent on us. Your parents may have been young when they had you. If that is the case, they were essentially growing up with you. If your parents, like mine, were older, they are not able to do as much and can develop health problems while your children are still young. That creates greater difficultly in helping them while balancing your work, family, and friends.

The common thread everyone shares is the need to maintain balance with everything going on in our lives. In the journey through our all-consuming life, it becomes a challenge to stay on an even keel. We get consumed with raising a family, working, and keeping in touch with everyone. If we add in caring for a loved one, we need more time. No matter what time zone you are in, there are only so many hours in a day. Time does not stop but keeps moving. Life's activities during this period are at a high level, garnering many challenges.

There is the struggle to keep balance in your life and maintain control over what is happening. This is something most want and will go their entire life trying to accomplish. The bottom line is that we do not have control over everything. I continue to strive to let go of the things I do not have control over. In my estimation I have been marginally successful. It requires ongoing mental reminders that it is not necessary to be in control every second for things to work out. There is tremendous freedom in embracing that reality.

Family

Family is the rock-solid foundation to live by. Through generations our families come together and help one another to grow and become strong, loving people. We use all the skills we have learned to integrate into society. Life is a gift. As our family ages, there is no greater honor than that of caring for an elderly member. It is easier to do nothing versus dealing with issues that require fortitude, energy, and love. The person/s we care for should not be dismissed or disregarded but embraced.

Their experiences from such a different time are an education for us about life and living. What they have seen, heard, and witnessed is part of our history. What better way to learn than by seeing and hearing about that history firsthand? They embody what makes us who we are today. There is the reality of life and how we approach it. Attitude is all about how we deal with life's ups and downs. Nothing in life has meaning unless we attach meaning to it. This meaning gives us strength to do the right thing and forge ahead.

As a Christian, I celebrate All Souls Day. It is a reminder of all those who have died and a time to reminisce about the good and special times we had with them. These memories include how much our life has been enriched by them over the years. It is a day to think about all we are grateful for in our life. I am thankful for my parents and ancestors who provided the groundwork and foundation enabling me to evolve to where I am today. Our parents brought us a good life. That is something to remember each day, not only on All Souls Day.

It is a godsend, even with the conflicts that arise, when our loved ones are alive—and difficult when they are gone. If you are caring for a loved one, there are times of feeling as though the weight of the world is on our shoulders, with no relief in sight. The task of helping a family member with their activities of daily living (ADLs) can seem overwhelming. There seems to be no light at the end of the tunnel. If your loved one is in grave health, you know that person is close to dying, whether it be today, tomorrow, or down the road. The journey comes to entail one day, one minute at a time. All those feelings of being lost and deflated start before the person dies and stay with you.

There is a difference between sympathy and empathy. Sympathy can cloud your judgment. It can hinder critical decision making. Each circumstance that presents itself at that time requires some forward action or nonaction. When the person is suffering, in pain, depressed, or experiencing the physical inability to function and/or any restriction on living normally, you can offer a measure of relief by just saying "I am sorry you are suffering. I understand the thing that is most important to you has been taken away." You are acknowledging that you cannot make the person better but asserting that you will help in whatever way you can. That is empathizing with that person. Sympathy is feeling sorry for someone, and that can prevent you from making sound decisions. Empathy allows compassion for that person and emotionally making the best decisions under the conditions presented.

In all stages of our lives, it makes a big difference to be grateful instead of dwelling on the things in our life that are not good in our mind. This helps us to look at others and ourselves in a more positive light. You may have heard the saying from your grandma or parents to "count your blessings." The bad issues will always stand out and the good take a back seat. It takes an everyday conscious effort to be grateful as a child and adult. The exercise of making gratitude a regular practice eventually sticks and has an escalating affect on how we feel about ourselves and others. Both neuroscientists and psychologists have conducted research and studies that show counting our blessings with focus and specific examples create a happier, more productive life.

There is not an absolutely right way to raise a child or care for a parent. There is no specific book that will give all the answers. Those answers are inside us. The opportunities, roadblocks, failures, limitations, and opportunities are what impel us forward in our life. Many times, we are faced with gray areas in which answers are not cut and dry. The key is to try to do what is right. We will make mistakes along the way. Those mistakes are the building blocks to grow and persevere.

Minute Meditation by Franciscan Media
FEBRUARY 16, 2017

Father, grant me the grace to take Jesus seriously and trust him to always be by my side and in my heart when I am beset by disturb-

ing problems that threaten to destroy my peace of mind and spirit.
I ask this grace in Jesus's name, Amen.

—from *Stories of Jesus* by Joseph Zimak

Children Growing Up through the Years

In the all-consuming life of raising a family, keeping in touch with
family and friends, along with caring for loved ones, it is difficult
to maintain a balance. It is at such a time in life that all undertak-
ings seem encompassing and challenging. That is, until you get to
the next venture. Issues can grow more complicated and serious.
Babies rely solely on you to care for them. The same holds true as
we age or endure a health debility, requiring us to rely on someone
else to take care of some or many of our needs. These activities include but may not be limited to eating, drinking, bathing, dressing,
walking, speaking, and all it takes to maneuver through the day.
This is the same for younger adults who cannot care for themselves.

As babies grow into adolescents and then teens, we are respon-
sible for providing a nurturing, caring, and loving foundation from
which they can grow; become independent; make their own decisions; and hopefully become happy, ethical, strong members of
society. The difference between a baby and an elderly or disabled
person is that the child has the potential to grow, while the individual in decline does not always have that privilege.

In our case, all four of our children were diagnosed with attention deficit hyperactivity disorder (ADHD). They went through
testing by a psychologist, with the recommendation to take medication. Although I was not professionally tested, I, too, have the
traits of ADHD. We were in constant contact with their teachers
over the years and monitored their progress. I read books and did
research. Who wants to give a young child medication on a regular
basis? The medication for ADHD is a controlled substance requiring close monitoring that has side effects. Although taking medication was the last course of action we wanted our children to take,
we decided to move forward with it. It did help. It was not a cure.
Improvement involved a combination of many measures, including
our children's desire to help themselves.

Dealing with our children's ADHD was one of the unplanned elements in our family journey that required ongoing monitoring and attention. Add in caring for others, such as your parents, and it takes a lot of effort and energy to balance your own home life and that of your parents. By itself, child raising in grade school, high school, college, and beyond requires much juggling. Our youngest son many times would have to come home to an empty house because I had to make an emergency trip to the hospital for my uncle, mom, or dad. I would leave him specific instructions. He knew he needed to finish his homework; study; maybe do a job around the house; and, of course, have a snack. I checked on him regularly. It was not an ideal situation. But our youngest son matured and is wiser than his years because of all he saw and heard.

Although we did not stop working, I resigned from outside employment when our third of four children started school so I could be home with them. As "the mom" volunteer for pretty much everything, I knew the teachers and students and got feedback by being around so much. That decision, unbeknownst to me at the time, led to another mission. These circumstances allowed my availability to care for and oversee the wellbeing of family members besides our own children. This was a calling I was fortunate to fulfill.

One of our son's birthdays is a special celebration for many reasons. He was yet another miracle child and is such a blessing. My husband and I worked on providing a nurturing environment for our children. There were obstacles and normal growth curves for us as parents and on our children's parts. There were times when we as parents felt like failures.

Things did not come easily for our children, and particularly for this son. He overcame being bullied and shunned by schoolmates in grade school, almost failing the fourth grade because of his ADHD. He could not retain information and was not doing well in school. Added to that, he had allergies that gave him a constant year-round runny drippy nose that provoked more teasing. He was noticeably quiet and could have been a child who fell through the cracks. This trait did not depict a typical child with hyperactivity. Although he was extremely busy, he was unobtrusive and rarely got into trouble in school. Whether the individual is a child or an adult, circumstances are not cut and dry, and each person's behavior is different, including how they react to their environment. As I mentioned before, the last route we wanted to take was putting him on medication for ADHD and allergies, but we felt as though we did not have a choice.

It was heart-wrenching to see him struggle. As a parent, you want to protect your child. We did not give up but kept working with him. We hired a speech therapist, availed ourselves of assistance within the school, and tried anything to help him cope and correct the ongoing issues. It was emotionally and psychologically difficult for him. He had some rough years. A great outlet was his participation in sports, including basketball, soccer, cross country, and track. With family support; outside help; and, predominantly, his hard work, fortitude, and never-give-up attitude, he is now thriving as an independent, successful adult. His struggles, as with anyone's, did not stop as he grew older, but our son learned to manage himself without medicine. He has acquired confidence in himself.

College Challenges

College encompasses learning, socializing, and maturing. It is an extension of your home. It is meant to be a healthy learning experience. We send our children care packages and go to visit them, and they come home for breaks during the summer and many times throughout the school year. Especially if the college student is within driving distance, they try to bring their dirty laundry home! This is my pet peeve. This is coming from the person who goes out of her way to help her kids. There should in my view be a stipulation that the college student does their own wash. College instills independent thinking and doing, but only to some extent. It is not until they get their full-time job and move out of the house that they are truly independent.

A college campus offers exposure to different ways of thinking and living outside the family setting. The campus is like an oasis all its own. It is up to the student to decide how much they want to get out of the education that is provided. As a parent, you want the learning part to come first and everything else to be a secondary but hopefully beneficial extension of good experiences.

Two of our children were resident assistants, providing free room and board. This cut down their expenses. They all worked before and during college to pay for their schooling. Our family believes in having the least amount of debt possible. It is not reasonable to come out of school shouldered with an exorbitant amount to pay back. Community college is a way to go to save on the cost, but any route chosen is a means for them to spread their wings. Sometimes those wings get clipped.

When one of your children gets into legal trouble, the result can be disastrous. This happened with us. We sent our children to schools we believed exemplified an extension of our values. They had experienced a solid upbringing in a close-knit family. Our children were not handed everything on a silver platter. Any money they earned went toward college, teaching them responsibility and ownership of their future. Overall, we thought our children were well grounded. What happened? What did we do wrong? The freedom of being away from home with nobody to answer to can bring out the wild side of a person.

In one of our children's cases, there were encounters with campus security on the first day of orientation. Problems arose through those first few years. College means different things for different people. Some want to get away from home, obtain a degree to pursue a career, while others are not sure what they want to do with their life and attend college as the thing to do. With the freedom to make your own choices, college life can become a big, ongoing party with drinking, drugs, and exploring. Some children and adults must learn the hard way with all those twists and turns that can be hard to maneuver. My husband and I prayed a lot.

Years later, thank goodness, this child got through those college years, ended up receiving a bachelor's degree with honors, and then graduated with an MSA degree. He now is a successful business-man. Early on, he took a fork in the road that led him down a dark path, but with support, perseverance, and hard work he has become a success. It is a great feeling to have a child graduate from college, receive a graduate degree, and pursue a successful career.

My son and I recently talked about his ADHD, mine, and our family's. It never goes away. He stopped taking medicine in college. That could have created some of the conflicts he endured—not to make an excuse for his behavior and poor decision making. It is still a constant struggle for him to stay focused. He works extremely hard, is tremendously competitive, and pushes himself to be successful. We are thankful that he got through that period and came out a stronger and better individual. The road was not always smooth or straight, but it did point in a good direction.

Nice Surprises

I received red roses from this same son. Never in a million years would I have expected that. It was not my birthday or any specific occasion—he did it just "because." It is special when unexpected, nice things happen. The card companies and the florists say that certain days are special, which they are, but that does not mean we have to follow what they promote and advertise. Every day is special. We try to make another person we care about feel loved. If I received flowers regularly, it would become a common occurrence and not mean as much. Now two of our sons live together and will send me flowers at random times. This is so appreciated.

Our One and Only Daughter

My husband and I could not have imagined what our beautiful daughter would become based on how she was growing up. We did not have immense expectations. She was rebellious and continuously against all authority figures. She even acknowledges now, "I was terrible in high school." This is not to mention the college years with her siblings! Our children went to Catholic schools from first through twelfth grade. We were fortunate that we could do this. It was important to us. We did not take trips, go on expensive family vacations, or spend excessively on material things, so we could put our money toward their education.

A shining characteristic about our daughter, from a young age, is that she always wanted to help people. She helped her siblings. If they were struggling with schoolwork, she could explain and motivate them. She helped her brother with his schoolwork and even helped potty train her youngest brother by seven years. This was a big help for me as a parent.

When she was in college, she decided to become a Certified Nurse Assistant (CNA). One must go to classes and take a state test to become certified. We found an accelerated course that was held during her Christmas break. The location was in a rough area. I decided I would take the class with her so I could protect her! She really did not need protection and could have taken care of herself just fine. This, however, turned out to be a great thing we did together. My daughter excelled in the course and was a sponge for learning medical terminology. She had a natural way to treat and care for patients. We passed the certification process. She passed with flying colors. I, on the other hand, was a wreck taking the course and going through certification!

Although the role was not exactly suited to me, I worked as a CNA, caring for a gentleman who was diagnosed with Parkinson's disease. He was rather difficult and not compliant with doing anything. The work was demanding for the few hours I was at his home, but it felt good to help. My dad, about whom I talk in a later story, had Parkinson's, so I was familiar with this disease and its effects. It takes the right type of person, one with a kind and giving heart, to work as a nurse assistant. There is no glory and not enough compensation.

Our daughter, in part, made her career choice based on her experiences helping to care for her grandparents and her job in college. When she was an undergraduate, she got a job at the university in a research lab. She really liked biology and wanted to follow a medical career. Thank goodness for that job, the doctor, and the research team she worked under. I am not exactly sure what type of research they did, but it planted the seed to become a doctor. The head person was a big influence in her decision to pursue a medical career.

She went on to medical school and is now a general surgeon

finishing her residency. That was not a path she would even have considered when she started her college career. There was not a straight path but many curves that led her to this decision and career choice. It was particularly difficult for her to study and take the required tests. The ADHD does not go away as a person matures, so a continuous, disciplined, concerted effort on our daughter's part was needed for her to succeed. She still must take her final board. The journey has been both grueling and fulfilling for her. Add in ADHD to the equation, and everything becomes more of a challenge. She was asked to be the chief resident, which is a testament to her work ethic and dedication. Like her siblings, she has worked extremely hard.

Our children could have taken a different course. There was no one specific thing that got them to where they are today; it took a lot of prayers, love, hope, family influences, and their own will to succeed. The fact that they had ADHD did not stop them—they persevered. My husband and I are enormously proud of them and what they have accomplished. We are thankful to be blessed with our children. Life will continue to present obstacles, but they have the will and faith and know the power of prayer to get them through difficulties.

Minute Meditation by Franciscan Media
OCTOBER 9, 2019

What Can We Learn from the Mystics?

The mystics teach us that one who tries to know and loves God sooner or later becomes aware that God is unknowable, but one can love God intimately despite God's ultimate unknowableness. With this awareness comes the further realization that all one's desire to know and love God has from the beginning been God's work and that, try as one may, two things are certain: You cannot find God, who has already found you, by running away from yourself, your own problems, your own unresolved fears; and secondly, everything you leave in order to respond to God's love is in the end redeemed, transformed, and given back to you wholly new and in an unpossessive way. It is as if you have returned to the garden or paradise illumined and purified so that you can walk again with God in the earthly paradise God intended for you from the beginning.

—from the book *Mystics: Twelve Who Reveal God's Love* by Murray Bodo, OFM

CHAPTER 2

The Legend of a Man: From Entrepreneur to Alzheimer's Disease

S EBASTIAN, BETTER KNOWN as Yonno, was born on February 26, 1915, in Detroit, Michigan. He was my uncle. There were twelve members in his family, with him being the fifth oldest. His parents, Joseph and Francesca, immigrated from Italy. His father was a peddler of fruits and vegetables, making about ten cents a day. He also delivered potatoes and other fruits and vegetables to schools with his sons. His wife stayed at home. She cleaned, took care of the kids, cooked everything from scratch, and took in wash and ironing from outsiders to earn needed funds for their family. With all the demands at home and the financial limitations, Yonno completed only eight years of school. When he was seven years old, he also sold newspapers on Jefferson Avenue in Detroit for one cent; he received half a penny per newspaper.

Yonno moved out of his parents' home when he was a teenager. He took with him his hard work ethic and motivation. He still wanted to be a part of his family and would visit them as often as possible. He was an entrepreneur who opened his own diner in Detroit, Michigan, on Jefferson Avenue, called Yonno's Place. He was the owner and head chef, with help from his brothers and sisters. It was a popular establishment for the policemen whose station was across the street, families, soldiers who were home on leave (this was during World War II), and visitors to the town. Yonno was known for his delicious homemade dishes; his pies had the flakiest crust. He said the key to a successful restaurant was good quality food, but most important was having excellent hot coffee.

After he sold his restaurant, he started a rubbish business in Detroit. His company, Commercial Removal, was the first privately owned rubbish business in Michigan. Along with picking up trash, he found a way to take care of snow removal. Yonno decided he would plow the streets of Detroit. There was a large quantity of snow in the winter months. Where do you put all of it? He purchased a truck with a plow in the front to push the snow, which he pushed or plowed into the Detroit River.

Yonno was very innovative. He had commercial clients and did residential trash removal for cities. His business grew. Over many years he added additional cities to his list of clients, both residential and commercial, growing his business to become very profitable. He brought other siblings and family members into the business, with some becoming part owners. They owned this business for thirty years and then merged two different times with larger trash removal companies.

Over the years Yonno remained close with his family, especially his sister Domenica, or Mary; that I will expound with her story. When I was growing up, Uncle Yonno would come to my parents' home regularly. I grew up with him as a positive, nonjudgmental figure in my life. He participated in most of our family functions and enjoyed food and eating.

When I got married and had children, Uncle Yonno continued as a part of our family and enjoyed talking with my husband and children. Our youngest son, Eric, saw him frequently. Eric grew up with him always being around. He would ask Eric about school and reiterate how important it was to get a good education. On Eric's days off, we took Uncle Yonno to the movie theatre. We got him popcorn and a Diet Coke. He loved it. We all enjoyed it. We saw mainly comedies. Eric helped him with everything, even going to the restroom at the theatre in Uncle Yonno's later years.

In the last twenty years of his incredible life, Uncle Yonno developed Alzheimer's disease and diabetes. There was always something happening with him. Unfortunately, there were quite a few hospital visits for various reasons. When he lived on his own, he went into diabetic shock due to his blood sugar levels dropping dangerously low. In this instance, I had been calling him on his phone, but he did not answer. My husband and I drove there and found him in a coma-like state, sitting in a chair. We thought he was going to die. The ambulance came and took him to the hospital. He got through that and became known as the man with "many lives!"

In his last ten years Yonno became very paranoid. He was also a hoarder! It was getting more difficult for him to take care of himself. He agreed to move to an assisted living facility. I had to get his house ready to put on the market. To list his home was an undertaking. It was not clean, and there were massive amounts of papers, old clothes, and even returnable cans. Yonno kept everything and would not throw out anything! He must have had 1,000 pieces of paper and mail stashed everywhere! I filled garbage bag after garbage bag. It was necessary to do some deep cleaning just to get his home on the market.

Yonno was reasonably agreeable about my going through his belongings and throwing things out. I would ask his permission so he would feel comfortable with me handling his possessions. He was moving from a five- to a two-room home. I had to get rid of a lot. A year later, the house finally was sold at a reduced price. Then came the move, which went well. Many times, older people—or others, for that matter—have a hard time adjusting to change. Yonno was excited about moving to a different place. A big part of the reason was to get away from someone whom he was certain was stalking him! Part of the paper trail that found its way into the garbage bags had pieces of paper with this person's name, and some included a telephone number.

One of Uncle Yonno's obsessive fixations was over a person whom I could never trace, named Gary Fincher. Gary Fincher remained in his mind and life for many years. Gary would purportedly take things from my uncle. The items Gary took were not usually of any great value— such as his tie, socks, or an extra, empty wallet. These were among a few of my uncle's disappearing belongings. Gary was a character my uncle honestly believed existed who was after him and his possessions. He had extreme anxiety over this.

When Gary Fincher came into Yonno's mind, there was no convincing him that Gary did not do the things he thought had happened. He would call me and the police. This happened day and night. He would be in an agitated state, demanding help. I went quite a few years believing Gary existed and even tried tracking him down. At one point the police said they could not keep going to his residence because it was taking them away from other emergencies. I had an investigator look for this fictitious individual to no avail. We had to conclude that Gary did not exist.

Over the years I would tell my uncle that Gary had been arrested and put in jail. Forgive me for not telling the truth! This worked for a time, but Gary kept coming back! This was real for my uncle and a recurring nightmare for me. Yonno had been a man who was always the most genteel, happy person you would want to meet. He would help anyone. Gary, if you are out there in the world, please return those items! An indication that Gary did not exist was the fact that I found some of the items Gary had supposedly taken hidden at my uncle's home. Unfortunately, his obsession with Gary did not stop after he moved.

We would go for months being okay, but once Yonno fixated on Gary, it was impossible to get him off that track. I would have to do something. I moved him out of two different assisted living facilities that were across a parking lot from each other times over the course of four years! Thank goodness he did not have a lot to move. In his room, he put a table in front of his door so Gary could not get in. This posed a problem because we could not enter, either. I was thankful that the table was small and could be pushed aside.

The assisted living residence was understanding and tried to help Yonno feel at ease. The food was good, which was important to him. He would go for walks to get exercise. Fortunately, he did not get lost. He loved to take walks. One of his walking trips was to the bank to check on his account and make sure no money was taken. The bank personnel knew him well. When he could not walk there, I took him and got to know everyone at the bank. They were accommodating and would spend time with him. That did help to ease his mind.

On another instance requiring a hospital visit, Uncle Yonno went to the hospital for dehydration. We thought he was not going to make it through the night. They gave him intravenous fluids, and he revived. In having routine blood work done, the doctors discovered that Yonno had a form of cancer, myeloproliferative disorder. Chronic myeloproliferative disorders are a group of slow-growing blood cancers in which the bone marrow makes too many abnormal red blood cells, white blood cells, or platelets, which accumulate in the blood. The oncologist explained that sometimes the disease progresses slowly and requires little treatment, while at other times it develops into acute myeloid leukemia (AML). Another setback for the poor guy. This doctor said that he would not likely die from this but from something else. He put him on a pill and regularly checked his blood levels. The doctor was correct; fortunately, the disorder did not rapidly progress.

Moving ahead a few years, I received a call from the assisted living place. The manager said Uncle Yonno was out of it, told them his stomach hurt, had no physical strength, and was very pale. I called his doctor, who recommended he go to the hospital. The emergency room doctor did an exam and x rays. They found he had a perforated, bleeding ulcer. The peptic ulcer is an open sore in the stomach lining or the upper part of the small intestine (duodenum). An ulcer can go through all the layers of the digestive tract and form a hole (perforation). Yonno's perforation was causing food and digestive juices to get out of the digestive tract.

Yonno needed surgery immediately. It was a critical situation. I stayed at the hospital through the night. The doctors came and talked with me three different times. asking about Do Not Resuscitate Orders (DNR). My husband was in New York, and we talked over the phone, which was not quite the same as in person, but it helped. The situation was scary. I prayed and asked to make the right decisions and that he would get through this. I asked the doctors to do all they could but not to resuscitate. Due to the blood loss, he required many pints of blood. Yonno got through that. He was ninety-four years old. His survival was a miracle. I was grateful the hospital had an adequate blood supply. If they had not, or the surgeon had said they could do no more, he would have died. After that, I decided to donate blood, which I have been doing for many years. That hospital is the same one in which my daughter is now a surgeon. It is a small, incredible world.

With the hospital visits came rehabilitation. Yonno had to stay for up to two months at the rehabilitation facility to recover and receive therapy. When he was in the hospital and rehab, I went daily to visit and to check on how he was doing and the quality of his care. During Eric's school days I would pick him up after school to visit. Uncle Yonno really perked up when he saw Eric. They were like long-lost buddies. In fact, all the patients loved to see Eric. Children usually evoke such a happy reaction from the elderly, not to mention other shut-ins. Eric was outgoing and interacted with everybody, bringing a bright spot to their day.

At the rehab facility, one of the exercises was to move small wooden balls, one by one, around a circular unit. Yonno would watch the therapist, and when he or she turned to see another patient would move a bunch of them. He was not normally sneaky, and we got a good laugh at that. It is good to have therapy to help in gaining strength, but someone with Alzheimer's does not see it that way and wants to be done with it. The person is like a child. We got a lot of laughs about this and other events over the years.

It was amazing that Uncle Yonno continued to have the physical strength of Goliath! On his last hospital visit he had fallen, requiring surgery for a broken hip. He was in a declining physical and mental state. When I was visiting him, he would repeatedly say, "Linda, get me out of here. I gotta get out of here." I assured him that he could leave soon. On one visit, I went into the bathroom for not more than three minutes. When I came back to his hospital bed, he was glaring at me. There was a pool of blood on the sheets.

He had pulled out his catheter and the IV that was in his arm and was moving to get out of the bed. The IV was tightly wound up and sitting on his tray.

The thought came to me he has never been that neat. Although what he had done was serious, it evoked both shock and laughter. How could he have done that? He just wanted to get out of the hospital! I had to schedule nurse aides to watch him when I was not there. The doctor ordered soft wrist restraints to be put on him. That was painful to witness, even though they did not cause pain; this was a solution to his trying to get out of the hospital bed and removing any medical attachments.

My son has his name, Uncle Yonno, embroidered on all his basketball shoes he has owned since high school. Uncle Yonno was the most caring and giving individual. He never complained. Although it was difficult for me to juggle everything, it was an honor that Yonno entrusted my husband and me to take care of him. He passed, along with the ubiquitous Gary Fincher, at ninety-five years old. Every day we feel his love, presence, and the warmth of that great big smile. He is a legend of a man who was larger than life and continues to inspire us.

Minute Meditation by Franciscan Media
August 4, 2017

What is God showing you that you are to do with your life? However small or great that is, it must be yours and not someone else's. What a stripping, for example, is sickness or aging, or the loss of loved ones, or ultimately the stripping that is the embrace of sister Death. The important thing is to give humbly and honestly of what God asks you to give. In the end you are the gift God wants; in the *meantime* each person struggles to know what God wants and whether one is really giving the gift of one's self to God.

—from the book *Enter Assisi: An Invitation to Franciscan Spirituality*

CHAPTER 3

Gone in a Flash: Mom, Her Daughter, Family, and Inspiration

I WILL GIVE A little background about Cecilia and her wonderful family. Cecilia and Joe had ten children. One of the couple's twins died from complications at birth. My husband, Jim, was the middle child. Cecilia and Joe had seven boys and three girls. They were a close-knit family that shared paper routes, tended a garden of fruits and vegetables, worked around their home, prayed, and played together.

Since the children's dad worked many hours, Cecilia pretty much did it all. She prepared the meals, sewed, canned, cleaned, handled minor home repairs, and maintained their busy household. She transported kids to school and did the grocery shopping with the one vehicle they owned, a station wagon.

MaryJo
At the top of this large family, the oldest daughter, MaryJo, or MJ, had epilepsy. She had frequent seizures, even with being on many medications. The other children grew up with MJ having these grand mal seizures. A grand mal seizure causes a loss of consciousness and violent muscle contractions, also known as a generalized

tonic-clonic seizure that is caused by abnormal electrical activity throughout the brain. Their family knew what to expect, but this was traumatic for her and everyone else.

MJ was close with her mom and dad. Her mom was her rock and foundation. Cecilia was a calm force who provided great support and who encouraged her daughter to be independent. When MJ was older, she moved to her own home and got a job. She was self-motivated and overall took care of herself. She was a deeply religious and spiritual person. Through her church she took pilgrimages to Medjugorje. We still have the holy water she brought back.

Since she could not drive, she would ride her bike to her parents' home, which was about five miles away. This did present a hazard. MJ was strong minded and felt she had a right to ride her bike on the road; unfortunately, she had some close encounters with passing vehicles! It was good to know that she at least wore a helmet. Some of the roads were terribly busy. If it were dark, her parents or a sibling would drive her and her bike back to her home.

When she was older, she went to Mayo Clinic and had brain surgery. This seemed to help with the seizures. My husband drove her yearly to Mayo for checkups. She was taken off some medications that had adverse effects on her personality. She did get better, worked, and continued to live independently.

Like my Uncle Yonno, she was very paranoid and claimed someone was taking her things. My husband and the police received numerous 911 calls about this. They were understanding and helpful in giving her some peace of mind. At one point the police told my husband that they could not continue going to her home, as this was taking them away from other critical situation calls. What is real and what is not can become unclear in one's mind.

Jim kept in touch with his sister. They usually talked on the phone once or twice a week. On one occasion, when she did not answer the phone after many attempted tries, Jim contacted his brother who lived in town. Terry went to her apartment, and after repeatedly knocking on the door he called the police, who had to break into her place. They found her on the floor, and she could not be revived. She was fifty-nine years old. That was a shock because she seemed to be doing so much better. We miss her and the example she set of working hard and striving to function to the best of her capabilities.

Cecilia/Mom

I think Cecilia/Mom was a saint in her own right. Cecilia was a source of unbridled love for MJ, her husband, her family, her extended family, and her friends. She was always supportive and worked extremely hard to keep this large family together. Even with all her household activities, she always took time to make everyone feel special.

I remember when I drove three hours, from Michigan to South Bend, Indiana, to meet Jim's parents over thirty years ago. I got to their home at dusk and rang the front doorbell. I was slightly nervous. The door immediately opened, with a man and woman standing behind the glass. The man, who looked imposing, opened the glass door and said, "Can I help you?" I introduced myself. The woman stood quietly. The man then said I must be at the wrong house! Yikes, my stomach dropped. The woman intervened with a smile on her face and said, "Hi, Linda. I am Ceil and this is Joe, my husband. We are Jim's parents." Joe said, "Hi Linda, I was just having a little fun with you." We sat at the kitchen table and talked for five hours. Jim came five hours later from Chicago, which is normally one to two hours away, through a blizzard.

My husband, Jim, was extremely close with his mom. She had been Jim's mentor and cheerleader when he was growing up. His mom offered encouragement and was proactive. Together we as a couple were close with his parents. Although we lived in another state, we visited regularly and always stayed in contact with them. From the moment I met her, she always made me feel welcome, special, and loved.

One week before Christmas we received a call from Mom and Dad. They told us Mom had lung cancer and that the prognosis did not look good. It was in her lungs and spreading. Her doctor presented her the options of undergoing surgery and chemotherapy or taking the nonaggressive approach of not undergoing further medical intervention. She decided not to undergo further medical treatment. Although she had been getting yearly checkups, we were always told all was fine; we believe the cancer had been in her body for years before she died. Ultimately, she did not survive her cancer diagnosis.

There had been signs that she was struggling. When we would ask her how she was feeling, she always gave a positive response. We could tell in the last few years that she was having a hard time with daily activities, that her health was declining. She went through her day-to-day activities and spent time with her family, especially her husband, Joe. They liked to travel and visit new places. My husband and I took a memorable trip to Belgium with them when I was seven months pregnant with our daughter. It was the best vacation we have had.

Mom lived life to the fullest, doing as much as possible for as long as she possibly could. It was only a matter of two months after we found out she had cancer that she died. In those final months, weeks, and days she remained positive; in fact, she was the most positive person I have ever met. She did not complain about anything during the twenty-five plus years I knew her. Within months of our finding out about her cancer, it had spread throughout her body and into her bones. She suffered in extreme pain those last weeks. We still to this day have a hard time grasping the amount of pain she must have endured.

A month and a half after the cancer diagnosis, Dad put her on hospice care. On a spur of the moment, we decided to travel from our home in Michigan to Indiana to see her. Hospice had set up a hospital bed in the family room, which connected to the door that went into the garage. This was the door we always came in when visiting. I can still see her face to this day years later. She was lying on the hospital bed with her feet facing that garage door. When she heard Jim and me say "Hi, Dad and Mom," on entering her home, she lifted her head, looked at Jim, and got a huge smile on her face. She had such a great big, sincere, beautiful smile. For that split second, her face became completely calm and focused, and she said, "Jim I am so happy to see you!"

At this point she was getting morphine every hour. You could tell the pain was still unbearable. She would hit her leg. She had to do something. This was a reaction that did not stop the excruciating pain. It could be marginally compared to slamming your finger in a car door; you shake your hand or maybe hold that finger tight. It does not make the pain go away but is a reaction to it. I cannot imagine this kind of pain. Jim's dad now questions whether she should have had more pain medicine. There are always lingering questions about what should have been done. I will discuss hospice in a later chapter.

On that Saturday Jim and his dad went to mass. Someone needed to be with mom, so I stayed behind. My job was to feed her an individual container of yogurt and administer the morphine after one hour. We did not get through the yogurt. I am not sure how she could eat this but was following my instructions. She could not communicate very much because she was in pain and in and out of consciousness. It was especially difficult and so sad to see her like that. I was crying inside but wanted to be strong for her. Her eyes were closed during this time. I asked her if she wanted to say the rosary. Mom looked at me and said "yes." I knelt next to her bed and held her hand. She did not say much, but I knew she was still with me; she remained calm through the twenty minutes that we prayed.

Jim and I stayed overnight. We slept on the couch in the family room for a few hours. Then Dad came into the family room and said he would stay with her, so we went to the back bedroom. I fell into a deep sleep. That night at 2:30 a.m. I woke up with a start. My heart was beating so hard and fast I thought it was going to come out of my chest! I had dreamt or envisioned that a black two-door car raced by me at an extremely high speed. I could see and hear it zoom by. It made a loud whooshing sound.

Our son, Mark, has a black two-door car. All my senses immediately registered high alert. My first thought was that Mark had gotten into a terrible crash! I jumped out of bed and rushed out of the bedroom into the hallway. Dad was walking toward our room. He said to me, "Mom took her last breath and passed away." That was the flash of the black car racing past me. Mom's heart had come to a crashing halt and stopped at the exact second I saw, heard, and felt the black car flashing by me. The sensation was so vivid and real I can still feel it today.

Our mom did not let this disease control her until the end, when it took over. It was not until the end that the cancer consumed her whole body, but it could not break through to her soul. She is an example of someone who had tremendous spirit and inner strength. I treasure her immensely. Your first reaction when finding out that someone has cancer is doubt and denial. We want them to stay here on this earth for as long as possible without suffering. We asked ourselves why this was happening. She did not deserve this. She was the most genteel, giving person you could imagine.

It was meant to be that we were there at that time. It is amazing how events transpire. By our going for that spur-of-the-moment visit, we saw Mom in her final hours, prayed, and gave her the peace of mind that it was alright to go. She was so concerned about Dad and what would happen when she was gone. Mom knew Jim would do whatever was necessary to help him. We stayed for a few days, helped with all the funeral arrangements, and gave our support. It was meant to be for us to be with them. My heart will always be with her, my mom and friend, Cecilia.

To this day my husband drives to spend the weekend with his dad, who is now ninety-two years old and still going strong. The daughter I was pregnant with on our trip to Belgium now has a baby girl with the middle name of Cecilia. She has the most beautiful smile, like her mom and great grandma, who is now without pain and smiling down on us.

Minute Meditation by Franciscan Media
FEBRUARY 9, 2017

Immeasurable Treasure

Tough times can be an opportunity to not only grow in Christ but an opportunity to help others who struggle with their ideal life. In human suffering there is an immeasurable treasure, and that treasure has the power to assist in the redemption of mankind.

—from *When You Suffer* by Jeff Cavins

CHAPTER 4

My Hero and Mom

THE PURPOSE OF writing this story is twofold. The first reason is to honor my mom, who did not go to fight in a war but fought a very tough battle to maintain her independence and dignity. She made herself get up every morning, eat, bathe, and get dressed, no matter how bad she felt. She always worked hard to help others, especially as a mom. It is extremely difficult to see anyone, let alone your parent, struggling so much. My mom tried every day to make the best of everything, like a hero. She had deep faith and love for her family that gave her an inner strength to push forward.

My mom had seventeen grandchildren, who all loved to visit with her and my dad. When visiting, she would always make sure you ate something. The table would end up being full of an assortment of foods. Of course, coffee was an absolute staple. Mom had so many stories and talked about many topics. She went to school through the eighth grade. She had to work with her family to help support everyone. She was a tailor, a seamstress, and an excellent cook. You would think she was top of her class in talking with her. She was incredible.

Music was always a part of our household growing up. My dad played the accordion. Before marrying my mom, he had been a professional musician. More about that with his story. They loved to listen to Sammy Davis, Frank Sinatra, Tony Bennett, Ella Fitzgerald, and all the other greats. My children would come with me to visit them when they were young, as well as on their own as adults, and through the course of the visit ended up dancing with her in the living room.

My mom changed her name to Mary when she was in school and thereafter. She was also Yonno, or Sebastian's, sister. In grade school, the other kids had a hard time saying Domenica and made fun of her. Thus, she called herself Mary. How she got Mary from Domenica is a mystery! She did not change it legally until way later in life, in her sixties. The name discrepancy created some legal issues, as you can imagine.

In her later years, we would help her with her bath . . . or more like shower. She would sit on a chair in the tub, insist on holding the handheld hose, and inevitably spray you down! I got as wet as she. We would talk during the whole shower, and she seemed to not notice. We tend to think the spraying could have been intentional! When helping her dry off one time, we talked about our surgeries. I commented that the scar on her stomach from a hysterectomy looked wide. She said, "It sure does; it looks like they used a serrated kitchen knife!" We had some good laughs.

We all have this remarkable desire to have our loved ones remain here with us, no matter what the cost. There comes a point in many situations when we may have to say "This is enough medical intervention. Now we need to allow life to take its course." My mom died four days after having surgery for congestive heart failure (CHF), on December 24, Christmas Eve, 2012. I think about her so much, and although it is not healthy to second-guess past decisions, she probably should not have had this surgery. At the time, the doctor assured us it would be successful. Her surgery did contribute to helping other patients with CHF (more on this to come).

I would like to give you a little background on my mom. She had many health issues. They had started about twenty years earlier, when my dad and mom were bringing my daughter, who was five, home from kindergarten. I was working at the time. My husband's sister, her husband, and their two children lived at our home for a few months while their house was being built. She would watch my daughter until I got home from work. Our doorbell did not work, so my mom went to the back patio to get Patty's attention in the kitchen. My mom tripped on a step and broke numerous bones in her foot. That is when they discovered she had osteoporosis.

Over the years she continued to fracture bones in her arms, legs, and especially her back. She shrank from a whopping five feet to four feet six inches over a ten-year period. She was in and out of the hospital and rehabilitation at the hospital. She would always fight her way back to being able to function. The amount of pain she endured is hard to fathom. In the later years, the nurses could not find veins to take blood, and she would be black and blue for weeks. Her skin became so thin. Medical intervention was traumatic to her body and mental constitution.

Through all of this she prevailed more times than imaginable. All of the doctors, therapists, and staff loved my mom. She was this tiny thing who was such a huge fighter. She would work at regaining her functionality. They marveled at her determination. My mom never looked her age, which always surprised them when they found out. She was ninety-three years young. Plus, she was sharp as a tack.

Through all these hospital visits and surgeries, she always seemed to maintain her sense of humor. My mom was extremely particular regarding how food was cooked. She loved cooking and baking and was exceptional at it. At home, she would leave the mixer on the counter, a self-proclaimed no-no, because she could not lift it to put it away. One of her passions was to cook. She influenced all her family and even the hospital she frequented. The hospital food left much to be desired. One comment she said about a piece of meat: "This is as tough as rubber!" She created a rapport with the dietician at the hospital, and after her many visits the menu changed. The food greatly improved.

As my mom got older, the hospital visits took a toll on her, both physically and mentally. It is true; each day in the hospital took away days from her mental and mechanical abilities. Like clockwork, it would be a year or less and something would happen that she would be back in the hospital, usually for weeks. Many of the times this was due to a fractured bone or bones that required her to undergo surgery. Thank goodness for a surgery called kyphoplasty that is like (but not actually) bone cement. She underwent this procedure ten times on her back. If she did not go through with the surgery, she would be in massive pain. The surgery and recovery are painful. The choice was always between the short-term pain with the surgery or continuous pain without it.

Sometimes her independent streak got the best of her. On one occasion, my mom fell and broke her hip, along with hitting her head on the counter, causing her brain to swell and bleed. I went to my parents' home almost every day. On this particular occasion she was lying down but got up when I came into their bedroom so we could have coffee. My dad was shaving. They were still mobile but not too steady. I poured coffee for us. I went to the dining room table, which is still part of the kitchen, and turned for a second.

My mom got up quickly (hoping I would not see her) from her kitchen chair, without her walker, turned toward the counter to get a spoon, got dizzy, and fell. I cannot blame her—I would have done the same thing. She needed that spoon to stir cream into her coffee and could not wait for me to get back. Or she simply wanted to get it herself. I should have had the foresight to make sure she had a spoon on the table. That split-second decision turned out to be disastrous. This fall was bad. I cried with my mom and said I did not know what to do. I tried to help her as much as I could, but it seemed as though it was not enough. It felt as though this was the last straw for both of us.

My dad was in the bathroom at the time. When he heard my mom yell and cry from the pain, he rushed out . . . and fell! He had Parkinson's disease and heart problems. What a disaster. I called 911. My mom had hit her head on the corner of the kitchen table, causing the brain swelling and bleeding that required a tube for the fluid to drain. She had also fractured her hip, which required surgery to have a rod implanted. It was a bad course of events.

How could I have let this happen? Taking care of parents, or anyone who is ill, is rewarding but also trying, exhausting, overwhelming, and emotionally draining. Since my parents did not want to move to an assisted living facility, we had family or hired help 24/7 for six plus years. I prayed to do the right thing. That is a whole different book about loved ones staying in their own home before going to an assisted living facility and finally to a nursing home. These options all have pros and cons, and the decisions depend on many factors.

Staying at the hospital took a toll on everyone. I tried to be there every day. I attended her occupational and physical therapy visits for encouragement, to stay on top of her progress, and to oversee her treatment plan. It is critical to have contact with the doctors, medical team, and nurses to keep abreast of everything. I found that the best approach is to be there early; many times, you can catch the doctor that way when he or she makes rounds.

When my mom was ninety-three, she had the last surgery of her wonderful life. This was for her severe congestive heart failure (CHF), and the surgery was called transapical arterial valve replacement (AVI). This procedure had just gotten FDA approval in December 2012. It is a less invasive procedure than the alternative, which is open heart surgery. There was no way my mom could have undergone that surgery, for sure. She was only the second patient to have the procedure done at the hospital she went to. The doctors assured us that it would go well and help her. They said she would feel so much better. She was tired and short of breath from any exertion. She would lie down during the day for about twenty minutes and then get up, ready to go. She was always active, whether at home or away.

During the prior year she had undergone tests to determine whether she was a good candidate for this procedure. The doctors first wanted her to have it done transfemorally (through a catheter in the groin), but with the curvature of her back, her petite frame, and her short stature, they could not perform the surgery this way. She had gone through a lot just to get to this point. She was leery of having the procedure done but signed on with my dad's consent, too. Many patients are on oxygen because their artery is blocked, and the blood is not flowing to the heart. Thankfully, she was not. However, it had gotten more difficult for her to do simple tasks, like bathing and walking. What was the right answer? The reality is that there could have been no absolute, surefire decision. We wanted her to feel better and did not want to let go.

The alternative procedure would open her aorta. We were told the risk was low, with a forty-percent likely success rate. We were informed that the outcome would in all probability be good, leaving the patient better off than she had been. She was struggling to do any tasks. Why would we not want to try to improve her quality of life? We talked with her primary care doctor, who was helpful but could not tell us yes or no. We weighed out all the options and decided to move forward.

The surgery took place on December 20, 2012. All our family was at the hospital. We decided not to bring my dad because we thought it would be too stressful for him. With his Parkinson's, he was very unsteady, unable to sit for long periods, and his symptoms got worse with stress. Once she was feeling better, we would bring him to the hospital. We were apprehensive but optimistic. After hours in surgery, the surgeon came out into the waiting room with his surgical gear on and announced that the surgery had been a success! What a relief! Mom went to the ICU, and we were told she needed to be taken off the ventilator before being moved.

From then on, however, her situation only went from bad to worse. She was bleeding from her mouth and nose. The medical team was not sure where the blood was coming from. Then they said that a piece of loose bowel had found its way into her stomach. It was a nightmare. The worst part was that the ICU nurse said we needed to be quiet and not talk to her to prevent her getting excited or stimulated. Some patients panic with the ventilator. She was sedated. The sad thing is that, had I known she was taking a turn for the worse, I would have held her hand and said I loved her . . . anything. It seems, looking back, as though the doctors already knew. They kept their distance over the next few days.

On Christmas Eve, I got called at 4:30 in the morning. I was on the treadmill, and my husband brought the phone downstairs and said the doctor from the hospital was calling about Mom. I had planned on showering and heading there. The doctor said that

Mom's kidneys were failing and that she would have to be placed on dialysis. I could not really comprehend or process what she was saying but responded with "How bad is this?" The doctor replied, "It does not look good, and you should come as soon as possible."

My husband and I rushed to the hospital. I called all my family, and we met at the hospital. My sister and her husband picked up my dad. The attending physician showed us into a private room and said there was really nothing they could do. He said that if she were his mom, he would not put her through any more and would let her go. We all cried. My dad finally had to see her with all these tubes. I whispered, "Please, God, do not let my mom die. Let her stay with us a little longer. We need her here with us. This is not the way to die." The nurse disconnected the ventilator and all the IVs. My dad sat and held her hand. Before the surgery we had thought this to have been the only option. The doctors had been so optimistic.

When they called and said she was scheduled for the surgery on December 20th, I asked the doctor whether it could wait until after Christmas. He said no. She would go off the waiting list, and they would not be sure whether or when she would have this procedure done. They had kept the pressure on. She had spent four other Christmas holidays in the hospital. We dreaded a repeat. We should have known this was a bad omen. Instead of saying we would wait and take our chances, we consented to getting this procedure done before it was too late.

A day prior and the morning of the surgery, my mom was instructed to take many baby aspirins. Her blood needed to be thin for the surgery. She weighed eighty-seven pounds. How could she take all those aspirins? No wonder she was bleeding so much after the surgery. To approve her as a good candidate, they put her through so many tests, poked and prodded. We should have raised the question about the quantity of baby aspirin to the doctor. All those second thoughts continue to come into play.

My mom was a case that did not turn out well. We wanted her to come out of the surgery and function better. Mentally, my dad and she were at a point that they could still make this decision on their own. We looked at all the options and together decided on the surgery. After weighing out the risks, we agreed it was a good option. Then there were all the complications: bleeding, not knowing from where it started; loose stools in her abdomen, meaning an intestine perforated; and kidney failure. The chain of events that happened after the surgery became a terrible journey. Within four days of her surgery, she died.

The surgery was performed successfully as far as the mechanics were concerned, but the outcome was not what the medical staff had anticipated. We must live with the fact of this unfortunate outcome. How can one ever know in advance the outcome of a surgery? The doctor was extremely optimistic and assured us our mom would have a better quality of life, with minimal risk. Otherwise, she would have only six months to live. A doctor really should not give a definite time a person will live. It may not go that way.

My mom was a treasure. She gave so much of herself. Her example of giving, caring, loving, and forgiving gives me the desire to go forward and do all I can on this earth. My mom left a lasting impression on her family, her grandkids, and all whom she knew. She was the glue that kept our family together. There is a void in my heart and a feeling of emptiness. I know my mom is here with me by a picture, story, recipe, and many other reminders that I see. My mom died on Christmas Eve. Christmas is all about family; the single most important driving force in her life was family. What better way to remember my mom, my hero at such a special holiday?

Minute Meditation by Franciscan Media
JANUARY 16, 2017

If we can attach meaning to our suffering, if there is some value in what we are experiencing, we can endure anything. Think about it. Nothing in Life has meaning unless we attach meaning to it.

—from *When You Suffer* by Jeff Cavins

CHAPTER 5

The Musician, Business Owner, Meat Cutter, Handyman

History of Phil

My dad, Phil, was a skilled musician, playing the accordion professionally starting at the age of seven. He played on cruise ships that traveled on Lake Michigan through his teen years. From 1939 through the 1950s he played as "Phil Gard" with one or two other musicians in Las Vegas. They were the opening act for Sammy Davis, Frank Sinatra, Dean Martin, Tony Bennett, Ella Fitzgerald, and other celebrities.

My dad was passionate about playing the accordion and had a pure, natural ability. He could play without reading the notes and wrote songs. After years of playing in Las Vegas, Phil returned home to help with the family grocery/specialty meat business, The Meat Center. He attended meat cutting school to become a butcher, then became an owner with his father and brother. This was certainly a different use of his hands. The best part of his return was that he met and married my mom. My dad continued playing the accordion at parties and family events.

The family business thrived for many years; unfortunately, they decided to close the store after it had been broken into and robbed three times. My dad then worked at a grocery chain in their meat department for some years but had to stop working due to his numerous health issues. He continued to be as active as possible, with music always being a part of our home life.

Health Issues

In 1984, the year before I got married, my dad had to have quadruple heart bypass surgery. He got through that. He continued to have heart blockages, enduring five stents over a ten-year period. The doctors could not repair some of the smaller arteries, requiring heart medication, monitoring, and later surgery to regulate his heartbeat with a pacemaker. It is incredible how things work out. We lived in Chicago the first year of our marriage, after which time my husband lost his job, spent months looking, and finally accepted a job in my hometown in Michigan. If we had not moved back, I would not have been able to help my family. I am fortunate in ways I did not know were possible.

Add to the heart problems, Dad was borderline diabetic, had melanoma (skin cancer), and had another skin disease, to name only some of the issues. Thankfully, my dad did not have to take insulin, but we had to closely monitor what he ate, and he had his levels checked regularly. He would develop UTIs (urinary tract infections), which added to his list of doctor contacts. He eventually needed 24/7 care. Since he remained in his home, I hired, fired, trained, and scheduled a total of eight people to help him, along with myself and three sisters, each of us with assigned days to stay at my parents' home.

My dad was diagnosed with Parkinson's disease when he was in his sixties. It was arduous to function with everyday tasks. Over the years things became progressively worse. If you do not have the disease or whatever ailment your loved one has, it is hard to comprehend what that person is going through, both mentally and physically. My dad became exhausted trying to carry out the simplest tasks. Everyday tasks such as showering, eating, walking, and talking required so much energy. These functions were physically and mentally tasking and required so much focus.

The History of Parkinson's Disease

Excerpted from *The Wall Street Journal*, Saturday/Sunday, September 9–10, 2017.

by *William F. Bynum*

James Parkinson (1755–1824) was a doctor who had Parkinson's disease. He was from East London and a general practitioner. Ms. Cherry Lewis wrote a book that is a bibliography on James Parkinson. The title, *The Enlightened Mr. Parkinson*, by Pegasus. He had the starring role. The most important words he ever wrote identified with his characteristic acuity, a notable feature of Parkinson's disease: "Shaking Palsy. (Paralysis Agitans.) Involuntary tremulous motion, with lessened muscular power, in parts (limbs) not in action and even when supported: with a propensity to bend the trunk forward, and to pass from a walking to a running pace: the senses and intellects being uninjured." The gait specifically is distinctive in the disease that we still call by Parkinson's name.

Added to the Parkinson's, my dad had melanoma. It required surgeries and constant monitoring. In the last year he went through Mohs surgery. Below is a description of the surgery and the physician who invented it.

Frederic E. Mohs, from Wikipedia

Text under CC-BY-SA license

Frederic Edward Mohs (1 March 1910–2 July 2002) was an American physician and general surgeon who developed the Mohs micrographic surgery (MMS) technique in 1938 to remove skin cancer lesions while still a medical student at the University of Wisconsin–Madison. The Mohs procedure is considered the best method for treating certain types of skin cancer because it has high cure rates.

Along with the skin cancer, he had another skin disease called bullous pemphigoid. This was a new diagnosis I had never heard of but rather common with the elderly. Even though I am not a medical person, the terminology became a part of my vocabulary after years of tackling this and other health issues with my loved ones. Bullous pemphigoid was horrendous. We were regulars at the office of Dad's dermatologist, who was fantastic. He was compassionate and always helpful.

This disease affects the skin, causing blistering, bleeding, tearing, and pain. It is an immunobullous disease. The blisters are due to an immune reaction within the skin. They were all over his body but predominately on his arms, chest, and upper back. It would take over an hour to treat and cover all the blisters. His skin itched, and my dad would scratch. He did not fully understand the importance of resisting the urge to scratch. We had to be creative in covering the areas so he would not scratch off the skin. We made sleeves out of socks to protect his arms. In the later years, it became more difficult to physically take him to the doctor. The dermatologist allowed me to send pictures, based on which he would give advice and prescribe what was needed.

Dad's heart and sugar issues were semi-controllable. The skin issues, especially the bullous pemphigoid, were not. The Parkinson's was the most debilitating. Along with Parkinson's came dementia. I do not know how, but my dad persevered. He was the strongest person; besides my uncle, I can imagine.

I think his physical strength came from his days holding the accordion, lifting sides of beef and pork at his meat store, plus the physical labor of doing projects around his own home and our families' houses. He was a terrific handyman who seemed to know everything about everything. My dad learned about plumbing, electrical work, carpentry, and handyman tasks from his dad. He completed school through the tenth grade. Along with these talents, he had a remarkable knack with numbers. It is amazing that without a formal education (not completing high school), my dad knew so much; he had an incredible mind.

To add to the pile of health issues, my dad suffered transient ischemic attacks (TIAs) in the last two years of his life. These attacks are also known as mini strokes and can be a precursor to a larger stroke. The doctor said there was no way to be one hundred percent certain that they had occurred and to be aware of what triggers these attacks, but it was highly likely my dad had them. He could have a medical exam, get a CT scan, and go through testing. My dad did not have physical signs after having these attacks, but it was clear that they altered his mental functioning. The question is whether it is important to put the person through testing to come to a firm conclusion that these attacks have occurred. The doctor did not think the testing was necessary. Blood thinners are normally prescribed. He was a huge fall risk so could not take blood thinners.

Days before my dad had a TIA, he would become hyperactive. There were signs before the TIA that were more telling than the actual attack. The body and facial signs were not visible because he was rigid from the Parkinson's. Two days prior to this attack, his behavior would become even more spastic, and he would compulsively touch and reach for everything. There were missions he pursued that even *Mission Impossible* could not have tackled!

Communication

Verbal communication is important, but nonverbal communication becomes critical if your loved one does not express himself. The nonverbal many times is more telling than the verbal. My dad spoke minimally, and as the Parkinson's disease progressed, he barely talked. He tried to answer questions you asked, but we could see it getting tougher and tougher for him to process any information. The best way to determine his condition was observing him to decipher all his quirks.

That hyperactive, impatient behavior carried through in all his activities. He walked with a walker, an activity that in itself was an unsteady venture. His body would be one foot away from the bars that he held onto because he was always in a hurry. My dad could not go anywhere alone. He was a moving safety hazard! If he wanted to lie down, we would walk to the bedroom, maybe do a lap around the couch, stop at the bathroom, and finally get to the bed. Then I would rush back to the kitchen to clean up or go to the laundry room to put in a load of laundry.

The thought that he was exhausted and would rest for maybe a half an hour was destroyed when he decided to get up after five minutes! He would not only get up but leave the walker behind and get maybe halfway through the bedroom. I even put a rail on his side of the bed, along with an alarm. That did not stop him! It was like the second coming of someone possessed by something! He either forgot about using the walker or decided he was going to try this on my own, without the assistance of the walker. He was like a child who attempts many things without thinking of the consequences.

Unfortunately, this sometimes resulted in a fall. I got a lot of exercise running through the house. Thank goodness it was not a large area to cover. If someone were watching me, they would probably have said I was the one with the problems! If speed and luck were on my side, I would get there before he fell. If he fell, it took an act of God for him to get up. Generally, he could maneuver himself to get up if he were not hurt. It was good for his mind, body, and spirit to have him help in the process. He already felt bad that he had fallen. This way he could do something on his own. The negative action turned into a positive.

Although my dad was not diagnosed by a professional, he had numerous signs of obsessive-compulsive disorder (OCD) that got worse as the Parkinson's disease progressed. Safety was an issue that escalated over time. It was amazing how someone who could not see well saw so much! If there were a crumb across the table or on the floor, of course he was compelled to pick it up. This was impressive and could only be attributed to early training that had stayed with him. He could barely move, but that crumb had to be picked up. I would jump and run to get the crumb before he did, so he would not have to reach or bend. That became another workout for me besides running through their condo.

The caregivers and I were always on high alert. Everything was exacerbated because of the dementia that came with Parkinson's.

He would compulsively move items one inch to the right or left. Aging, dementia, and other factors affects one's vision. There is some correlation between dementia and visual impairment. The brain is not functioning normally; in my dad's case, add Parkinson's to the mix to further diminish all his senses.

His health continued to decline. He was struggling increasingly more, and every function was becoming harder. It became harder to help him with the activities of daily living (ADLs). The one thing we did daily was listen to music. He loved to listen to all his favorites. It helped him to relax. We did not talk a lot but enjoyed listening to the music. He would get absorbed in the tunes and tap his feet on the floor. This was an innate instinct that he did not lose.

The Parkinson's disease and dementia progressed further as the years went on. He had this debilitating disease for over twenty years. Parkinson's is difficult in many ways. One becomes a prisoner in their own body. The disease takes control of the person. It is incredibly challenging for both the sufferer, whose body and mind are deteriorating, and the caregiver, who is seeing this and physically helping that person.

Dementia is difficult to diagnose. I saw how my dad fought it. He tried hard to function normally and, on some days, seemed his usual self. However, there was no "normal." Since he did not communicate much, that made it even more difficult to decipher what was happening with him at any given time. Careful observation on the part of the caregivers yields little signs they come to know.

My dad knew he was slipping, that tasks were becoming more difficult, without much hope for the future. He got depressed. I do not blame him. I got depressed, too. Every time we visited the neurologist, they would ask the question about being depressed. My answer was "Hell. yes! But no, we are not adding a medicine for his depression."

One of the signs by which I gauged how the PD was progressing was my dad's writing or printing. I got a notebook. It was the kind that young children use when they first learn to write, with the spaced lines between the solid ones. We used these notebooks when I attended grade school. Writing had been part of my third-grade curriculum. That is not the case today. As time went on, my dad's writing became smaller (more cramped) and less legible. The neurologist would also have him write as part of his examination.

Eating and Choking

Everyone has some passion for something. In my dad's case, it was family, music, and eating. He lived to eat. Unlike some people who are not well and lose their appetite, my dad never lost his immense pleasure with eating. His appetite did not wane, even with declining health. He had an almost voracious appetite. Even though he had such a good appetite, he lost muscle mass, making him thin and frail.

Another problem with PD is choking. This is one of the signs of the later stages of PD. It did not help that my dad ate fast. As time went on, the choking instances became more regular. He had to be watched very closely. It required creativity to help him. We constantly had to tell him to take smaller bites and chew his food. We would give him a little at a time instead of a whole plateful. We discovered that putting other plates or platters on the table with food was a mistake. If you did so, my dad would reach for everything and eat whatever was nearby. It was easier to see the plate above his own, so we moved his plate further up on the table.

The last choking instance occurred with my dad eating watermelon. Watermelon is easy to choke on because of all the liquid. Also, meat and things that are hard to chew and swallow can cause choking. My dad loved fruit. In this instance, the watermelon was found in pockets in his mouth between his teeth and gums. We had been to the speech therapist before and received helpful information on preventing choking. Although we were watchful and careful, it still happened.

This happened on a weekend when my husband and I were in Indiana to see his dad. My husband, Jim, has gone religiously every other weekend, from Saturday through Sunday, to visit and help his dad, who lives in South Bend, Indiana. I went with him this weekend; I was not always able to go because of our children and all their activities. The routine—every visit is about the same—

involves stories being told by his dad and some great talks; Jim puts a roast in the oven to cook before we head out for 5:00 p.m. mass. We have dinner together, staying through Sunday evening, with Jim making breakfast and dinner and then driving three hours home. Jim helps with anything necessary: cleans; does the dishes; and helps with financial, and many times computer, issues. My husband's dad is another beautiful story.

We were on our way home from South Bend when I received a call from one of the caregivers. Dad was choking on watermelon. She had to do CPR and had called 911. She was overwrought. We had other scares with choking but were able to help him by taking the food out of his mouth—or he would spit it out or eventually swallow it. In this instance, he could not stop choking. We talked for a minute; I felt terrible being two hours away and unable to do anything. I have rushed over to my parents' home for so many emergencies, but this time I was unable to get there quickly.

The Heimlich maneuver was applied on my dad by the caregiver. Medical professionals have told me that a person can sustain broken ribs when it is done correctly. One must compress his chest so hard to get to the heart that ribs will break. My dad sustained six broken ribs. The EMS stabilized him and transported him to the hospital. Once one thing happened, a chain reaction started.

My daughter was a resident Doctor of Osteopathy (DO) at this hospital, thank goodness. I told her to please tell the doctor not to give my dad Heparin. In caring for family and being at the hospital many times as a CNA, I have seen that the doctor automatically prescribes and the nurse administers Heparin. This is done to thin the blood so that blood clots do not form. The nurse injects the Heparin in the stomach several times a day. If you are not there to see this, you would not even know unless the patient tells you, you ask, or you look at the medical records or their stomach. The patient is already going through so much. Why have him go through this? Is it necessary for this patient? This is a gray area?

This choking incident was something you would think could have been avoided with closer monitoring and observation while he was eating. But this takes only one second to happen. Dad had

24/7 care with good conscientious help. He still experienced some falls and, as time went on, this choking problem. You run the risk of things happening no matter what you do to prevent an incident like this.

The easiest solution was to keep him in a wheelchair or bed and feed him. My dad was a high risk for almost any kind of mishap. He ate too fast, did not chew his food well, and was unsteady and a big fall risk. He had a lot of strikes against him. It became a daunting undertaking to keep him well and safe. The benefit of his staying as active as possible was that this kept him going. His physical therapist pointed out, "If you do not use it, you lose it."

There is a lot of common sense involved in caring for a person. It requires changing from what you think you know is best for that person to doing what your loved one conveys to you is best, based on their medical condition, mental status, and actions. This requires creativity and putting their interest in the forefront. I strongly believe that if we had not kept my dad as active as possible—walking, exercising, and interacting—he would have suffered more and died shortly after my mom did, years earlier.

My dad needed to get out of the hospital after the choking incident. He stayed there from Sunday to Tuesday. He failed the swallow test. He was out of it when they took him to do the test. How could he have passed? I am not sure he would have passed even had he been more awake—probably not. The speech therapist recommended a feeding tube as the best option. That was neither his wish nor ours. This all happened so fast. The doctor, who was a DO, was helpful and compassionate. He pointed out that we had some options. We could put Dad on a feeding tube, on hospice care, have him eat thick pureed food, or a combination of these options. We decided to go on hospice with the pureed food. Within a matter of a few hours, he went into hospice care.

Dad came home from the hospital. Surprisingly, he did well for about a week. The hospital is very tough on elderly people. They are taken out of their own environment. My dad needed his routine, to be in his home, and to take medications at the same time each day. according to the established schedule. No matter what I did to communicate with the nurses and doctor that he needed to take his Parkinson's medication promptly every two and one-half hours during his waking hours, this did not happen. I gave them the doctor's written instructions, but the nurses, with all their other patients, were unable to adhere to his schedule.

Could it be possible that Dad had another life in him and might get better? My sisters, the caregivers, and I gave it our best shot. We tried to concoct tasty pureed foods. We added sauce, juice, and seasonings to give it flavor. But these concoctions were not the same as chewable food, no matter how you spin it. At that point he did go downhill fast. Prior to this, taking care of him had been incredibly challenging, but now it was almost impossible.

He had all the other limitations, and now add broken ribs. With broken ribs, it was hard and painful to breathe. It is extremely difficult to see someone struggle so much. His breathing became more labored and diminished because of the broken ribs. We had him breathe into a manual breathing device and to move around while trying to get comfortable. I had the priest come, we said prayers, and he gave my dad a blessing This priest visited with my dad many times, which gave him some peace.

Hospice left a machine that suctions extra fluid out of the lungs, sending this with the other equipment but not asking us to use it or providing instructions. This is not exactly a time you are thinking of asking questions; you want someone to help you help your loved one so rely on them to give input. We did not know the signs of a person dying, and they did not give much direction as to what to do. It seemed almost as though the suction device were there as a prop. Maybe we should have called them more often and had them come to the home. Now that I think about it, it seemed as though they were not trying to relieve the pain but letting my dad go through the process without providing relief. It was my daughter and niece, who is a nurse, who instructed us on using the suction device, and we did utilize it.

Suction (medicine), from Wikipedia
Text under CC-BY-SA license

The portable suction unit of an ambulance

A dental vacuum system for central suction

In medicine, devices are sometimes necessary to create **suction**. Suction may be used to clear the airway of blood, saliva, vomit, or other secretions so that a patient may breathe. Suctioning can prevent pulmonary aspiration, which can lead to lung infections. In pulmonary hygiene, suction is used to remove fluids from the airways, to facilitate breathing and prevent growth of microorganisms.

Minute Meditation by Franciscan Media
MARCH 31, 2017

Consolation in Suffering

Most High, Glorious Body, in our times of suffering, may we follow the example of Jesus: but may we also serve as a source of comfort and consolation to others in their suffering. May we never let the fear of suffering stand in the way of our calling to love and work for justice. Amen.
—from *The Last Words of Jesus* by Daniel Horan, OFM

It was not hospice that gave Dad comfort but all the love of his family and caregivers. Hospice provided the equipment, hospital bed, oxygen, pain medicine, some instructions, and light monitoring, but it was my nieces, nephews, sons, daughter, and her then fiancé, who is now a CRNA (Certified Registered Nurse Anesthetist), who gauged Dad's medical status and decline.

I called the hospice person to come by Dad's home because he was struggling. I asked him what else we should do. That person did not offer much direction. With the help of Dad's caregiver, Shirley, and myself we washed him in the bed, put him in a clean white T-shirt, and changed his sheets. Shirley, along with all the caregivers, was a godsend to us. She was caring, kind, and knew what to do. She cared for my dad for many years and knew him well. We made him as comfortable as possible. Within twelve days of coming home from the hospital Dad passed away.

Shirley and my niece, who was a nurse, were both present. Over the course of the day, Dad had moved into the fetal position and was struggling to breathe. Is it possible to have a peaceful death? There is the inner struggle between life and death. We orient ourselves through our whole life to live and go through all the struggles on the journey. It made a difference, especially in Dad's final years, to have good, kind, compassionate people around. We are thankful for all that my dad helped us with over the years and so grateful he stayed with us for as long as he did. He was an example of selflessly providing for his family.

Minute Meditation by Franciscan Media
SEPTEMBER 26, 2018

She wrote about purgatory which, she said, begins on earth for souls open to God. Life with God in heaven is a continuation and perfection of the life with God begun on earth.

—from *Saint Catherine of Genoa Feast Day,* September 15

CHAPTER 6

Doctor Appointments, the Specials, Emergencies, and Hospice

T HE DOCTOR PLAYS a vital role in an elderly person's care. My parents had a phenomenal internal medicine doctor. His name was Dr. David Hug, he was their doctor for over twenty years. My mom frequently got sick with recurring issues, such as upper respiratory and sinus problems, vertigo, stomach problems, and bouts of high blood pressure. Dad and Mom were regulars at his office. He knew them well and would call them at their home with test results.

Dr. Hug was very compassionate. He treated them with dignity and respect. He gave them the facts so they could decide on a treatment plan. At the doctor's visits he would talk directly to them and explain clearly what was going on. In my dad's case, he did not advocate end-of-life aggressive measures. He cut back on their medications as they aged. He would listen to them and me. We called him before my mom had her CHF surgery. Although he did not tell us what to do, he knew my mom better than the doctors doing the surgery and could give a nonbiased opinion. He did not give false hope about that surgery.

Doctors' Visits and The Special

As a caregiver and someone who oversees a person's care, my objective was to have things run smoothly, maintain the patient's routine, and eliminate as much stress for them as possible. I knew my parents. If they knew in advance about an upcoming doctor appointment, it would cause worry; nervousness; and likely, on my dad's part, staying awake for most of the night prior to the appointment. He would keep my mom awake, too, with his moving around in the bed. He had bouts of nightmares, thrashing, and talking in his sleep. Then, if they had not slept well, they would be exhausted. My dad would have difficulty moving, along with increased unease.

Honesty is the best policy, but there are times when full disclosure backfires and causes tremendous anxiety. The ensuing day would only be more difficult. So best to not let them know ahead of time. The overnight person would make sure that morning that they went to the bathroom, had their medicine, brushed their teeth, cleaned up, shaved (in my dad's case), and had nice clean clothes on.

I would make an early doctor's appointment if they had to fast. No big deal you would think. Think again! For some elderly people, this is a disruption to their routine. In my parents' case it required planning and communicating with the overnight caregiver, while not disclosing these plans to my parents. My mom was a lot more adaptable and accepting of change than my dad. Dad was a worrier; the PD made it worse.

After the doctor's appointment, we would go out for breakfast. This was a treat for them and for me. Specifically, my parents loved going to a place called Ram's Horn. My dad would order the big "super special," with eggs; hash browns; toast; bacon; sausage; and, of course, coffee. As I had mentioned, he had a great appetite. My mom would order a much smaller scale version of the same. They loved their coffee, and someone was always coming around to refill our cups. That restaurant catered to the elderly. When I initially went to Ram's Horn, I thought to myself and told my husband, "I do not like this place. It is overpriced, not too clean, and not that good." I did change my tune. *Give them a break; it is only break-fast, right?!*

Over the years we got to know the servers. If the power went out at my parents' condo, it would be off to Ram's Horn to eat. As the years progressed, it became more difficult for my dad to eat. Sometimes he would use his fingers. Probably a quarter of the food was on his lap and the floor. I was constantly jumping up to catch a sausage or clump of egg that was falling. The restaurant servers and managers did not mind. This became a little time of respite for my parents and myself, and this continued for my dad years after my mom had died. They thoroughly enjoyed their outing, and it helped to make the day better. Even with the jumping, I could drink a cup of coffee and maybe make a few notes about the doctor's visit. It is so often the small things that add up to be of big importance.

It is good to document doctor visits. I do not have a great memory and did not trust it. With documentation I could check back. Over the course of time, my notes became a good reference about past medical information. Even though the doctor and corresponding hospital are supposed to have the patients records of all current and past information, it is not always accessible. For instance, what medication he/she is allergic to, when a prescription was stopped, whether he had a reaction to a medication, when he was in the hospital, and the list of his current medications. What were the doctor's instructions? This needed to be communicated to all the caregivers. I had an area on my parents' dining room table with a large calendar and notebook for myself and everyone else involved to write in. It was especially important for everyone to be on the same page.

There were times when we could accomplish the same result from the doctor by forgoing a trip to his office. Dr. Hug knew how difficult it was to transport my parents for their doctor visits. He made it as easy as possible. For instance, he allowed us to secure a urine sample at home and drop it off at the office instead of making a trip into the office. He would call with information. We could talk with the receptionist or nurse, who would relay information to the doctor, and either they or the doctor would get back with us to give a diagnosis and medical advice. If my mom got sick with the same symptoms as those from prior visits, the doctor would give his recommendations without insisting on her coming to his office. I was so grateful for that huge help.

The neurologist for my dad made available an online portal that I used regularly. I could send a message anytime, day or night. The assistant would convey the message to the doctor, and he would provide advice and guidance. I could send a message providing feedback on how my dad was doing after an adjustment to his Parkinson's medication or our trying a new one. There were always questions about drug interactions. At one time Dad was prescribed Metformin because his sugar was so elevated. My dad took it for about a week. He had a terribly adverse reaction; it did not mix well with his Parkinson medicine. We had to stop that medication. Another person with Parkinson's might have been fine taking it.

The next best resource after the doctor was the pharmacist and staff at our local drugstore. They got to know us by names. The pharmacist even called to see how my parent/s were doing. We could pick up prescriptions by going through the drive-through window. This was a big deal. We did not have to get them out of the car or worry about leaving them there so we could run in and get the order. The best place to get information about drug interactions is through the pharmacist. With all the pills my parents took, we called a lot. They went above and beyond what was required of them and really cared.

Sometimes the days are so busy it is hard to remember what day it is. The days blend into weeks. I would wake up and wonder what day it was. Was I the one losing my mind? With all the advances in medicine, we are living longer. Are all the pills such a good idea? You take one pill to help an ailment, and it has side effects that cause another problem. This interaction can be like a rollercoaster ride with many ups and downs.

The Hospital and Emergencies

Before my parents required 24/7 care there were many times when they called 911. The fire department and paramedics would come.

It is scary when something happens. They had always lived in their own home and relied on each other. The paramedics, as part of their protocol and for safety measures, ninety-five percent of the time insisted on going to the hospital. Even if Dad or Mom had become stable between the time 911 was called and the arrival of the paramedics, they would say that he/she should be taken to the hospital.

The EMS and fire department crew got to know my parents and were helpful and responsive. If my dad fell, my mom would try to help him up. That was a fiasco! My mom was so frail she could easily have fractured one of her bones. After years of coming to their home, the fireman would help him get up and not insist on having him go to the hospital. My parents were in and out of the hospital so many times over the years, and each time it took longer and longer for them to recuperate and get their strength back.

Hospitalization was disruptive to their daily living routine, emotional stability, and overall wellbeing. It was terrible, especially for my dad, because of the Parkinson's, dementia, the need to keep him as mobile as possible and to administer his medicine every two and one-half hours, and the effort it took for him to use the bathroom. We tried to get the help they needed to avoid the emergency trips. After my mom died, I talked with the doctor, and he respected our wishes for my dad to not go into the hospital. Dad stayed out of the hospital for over four years. He had the falls, choking instances, and TIAs to name a few emergency situations, but each time we managed to get him up and running.

Over time we had up to eight caregivers, plus family members, with each person handling emergency situations a little differently. As a caregiver, you are on the front line with each emergency and must make decisions and act. You must constantly adapt and change with the needs of the patient. I received numerous calls from the caregivers during the day and the middle of the night about an issue. This was unsettling and disruptive, but I needed them to let me know what was going on. Communication was key, and we could talk through what was going on and come up with a plan.

It was a battle getting help and a process to keep the caregivers employed. There was a lot of dissent from my parents, who did not want to go to an assisted living facility or to hire "outside the family" help. First it was a struggle because they did not willingly accept help even from their children. Then arranging for "outside the family" help was faced with even more opposition. They usually found something wrong with the caregiver. If it were up to them, they all would have been fired.

Time spent in the hospital could have been days or weeks if they required rehab. If one of the two was at home, the situation required double duty. It essentially required triple duty because you have the patient in the hospital or in rehab, the other parent back at their home, and your own family in need of your attention. It becomes a three-way consortium! More energy is needed, not to mention spiritual guidance.

Faith is the cornerstone of doing what is right and believing that, whatever the outcome, we had looked at all the possibilities and put our own personal interests aside to help that person. Of course, we made many mistakes along the way. Our initial decision was not always the thing to do, and we often found that another way worked out to be the better option. Everything is a work in progress. I hope and pray to always be humble in seeking the best way and for the Spirit to enable my decisions to be filled with the blessings of clarity and charity in all things.

At times, we need to go through many bumps, wrong turns, and misdirections in the road we are following. That road is not always as straight as we would like it to be. There are times we may think we cannot do any more or go any further. Then something happens to get us on the right track. Things have a way of coming around and eventually working out.

Minute Meditation by Franciscan Media
SEPTEMBER 9, 2017

I Will Give You Rest

In a world where people "look for love in all the wrong places"—

settling for second-rate substitutes that can result in addictions, family strife, depression, and suicide—Jesus shows us a way. He is the answer to all our questions, no matter what our age or state of life. He offers solace to those aching for relief. He offers truth to young people who are searching for deeper meaning and security. He restores the dignity and moral center of those who are looking for life and see only death. To each of these weary souls Jesus says: "Come to me, all you that are weary and are carrying heavy burdens and I will give you rest. . . . Learn from me; for I am gentle and humble in heart, and you will find rest for your souls" (Matthew 11:28–29).

—from the book *Healing Promises: The Essential Guide to the Sacred Heart*

Hospice

Hospice care is not meant to be a miracle that sweeps into your life. It is hard to find the right hospice organization that fits in with your circumstances and family. They are not all the same. There are so many hospice places to choose from, along with many options to consider based on your specific circumstances.

The best fit for your loved one is based on the organization's approach, along with the patient's specific needs and issues. I have talked with about ten different hospice facilities when interviewing them for my uncle and dad and seeing them care for others. Their overall mission is similar, but the people and amount of support varies from one place to another. I have also heard about relatives' and friends' experiences with hospice caring for their loved ones.

My husband's dad was told by the hospice person to give his wife a certain amount of pain medicine, which he followed. But her pain intensified over a short period of time. She suffered in extreme pain at the end; looking back, we realize she should have had additional pain medicine. An uncle who recently died went on hospice for five days, was in a peaceful state, and displayed no evidence of pain. Overwhelming pain can prevent the person from getting to the next stage, preparing for the transition to their passing.

Some of the hospice workers seem unaffected by dying and death. This is understandable, given that they have seen so much of it, but that does not help you. They are to some extent doing their job, but they can become cold and mechanical and lose their compassion. Even though the worker may be given pain medication to administer, it is too often set aside for later. In our case, the case manager put a stash in the refrigerator and said that it was only for extreme emergencies. I did not know what an extreme emergency would be and should have asked.

The experience of losing someone stays with you always. There are reminders that pop up. Thoughts come to mind at random times. Fortitude is what keeps us going. We may have others in our lives who still need our help. We need them around us, too. Our own resilience and everyone around us can provide the support we need to get through the difficult times and the strength to go on. Life is indeed a journey.

Pain

Being in a state of pain is exhausting. It is hard to maintain a good disposition. Years of suffering are totally draining. There needs to be some inner strength of spirit that keeps the sufferer going. In the case of all my family members and friends, the pain and struggles were softened by the love and support of family and caregivers.

If you have faith in God, it is easier to let go of things you cannot control and entrust them to God. This is much easier said than done. There are things we can control and others we cannot. Those we cannot control we need to place in God's hands. It takes the pressure off, provides some relief, and offers freedom.

Minute Meditation by Franciscan Media
FEBRUARY 17, 2014

Faith in Action

Faith is to believe what you do not see; the reward of this faith is to see what you believe.

—from *A 40-Day Spiritual Workout for Catholics*

CHAPTER 7

Dying, Death and Grieving

Dying Can Bring Terrible Suffering

Facing the fear of the unknown creates anger and anxiety. Everyone deals with death in a different way. Family members may become desperate and go to any extent to compel the person who is suffering to get better. Our emotions are running rampant; although normally we think logically, we may not see clearly. It is a false hope to make that person better; they are not going to get better. On the other hand, and I have seen it, you may think the person is knocking on death's door, but then they recover! It is like having a store of life that we do not see. It becomes tenuous and a fine line between living and dying. That is a time when we do not have control and must rely on our faith.

We can think of this as the eleventh-hour cavalry coming in to impart their ideas. Family members will interject their strong opinions about the direction of care to provide for this person. They may want your loved one to go to a different doctor; sometimes years after having a health issue. They push that maybe a different doctor can give another option, but it is late in the process. If the person is dying, no onetime doctor appointment or event is likely to make them better. Anything is possible, yes. It is good to be open, but sometimes a power struggle occurs within the family. The frame of mind to stay focused is best for the suffering person and invariably the right course of action.

It is not for us to predetermine or try to orchestrate the where and when of a person's passing. There needs to be some balance between hoping the person gets better or back to their previous level of functioning and knowing that they will not recover. Dealing with the facts and balancing your emotional ties with that person are like playing a constant game of tug of war with yourself. Is it possible to have a peaceful death? Is the best we can ask for to have peace? Hospice can help by using medication to take away some of your loved one's pain and providing other means to make them more comfortable.

As a Catholic, we are taught that we should not shy away from death but embrace it. The belief is that we will rise from the dead. I have a hard time grasping and embracing this, but, nonetheless, it is part of our faith as Christians. Fundamentally, in my personal paradigm, I picture us as living to die. It is in living that we can face death. From that perspective, seeing someone you love and care for suffer and die is hard. The process can seem cruel, unfair, brutal, and painful, but having some form of faith helps us get through it and be able to accept that our loved one has died. We need to go on.

When the person dies, all the activity that has revolved around them comes to a halt. Their presence in our world is gone. All the physical and mental energy to do everything necessary and possible to maintain their dignity is no longer needed. This has been a heavy weight for us as their caregivers and loved ones to carry around; we may have felt as though we were carrying the world on our shoulders. The wellbeing of our loved has to a large extent been in our hands. The load of responsibility gets higher and higher, until one day it collapses. If you have ever played the game Jenga, you will know that it is like that. You stack all the wood pieces on top of each other and carefully extract pieces, one at a time, trying not to make the other pieces fall. Eventually, the structure will weaken and tumble. Staying stagnant is not an option. There are so many variables that come into play that we cannot determine the beginning or ending to the story.

Grieving can cause immense sadness. On the outside, our appearance does not necessarily show our sadness. We go about our everyday activities as we normally would. I have tried to cope by filling the void and staying busy. The best way to describe this is motion in a state of fog. We go through all the motions of each day, but that sadness is within us. The grieving process is not the same for everyone. There are stages of grief (see next paragraph) that describe the mental steps of going through the grieving process. This model is helpful in a general sense, but grief is an individual, internal process that evolves as it will. Yes, time does blunt the pain, but it is still there. Reminders and mementoes are a good thing in that they help us to continue dealing with our emotions.

According to Elisabeth Kubler-Ross, there are six stages of grief: denial, anger, bargaining, frustration, depression, and acceptance. These are good guidelines. However, everyone grieves in their own way. Grief is not a single, fixed feeling or a set series of emotions. You need the inner strength to go on. The reality is that we will grieve in some way forever. You will not get over the loss of a loved one. You will learn to live with it over time. You will heal, and you will rebuild yourself around the loss you have suffered. You will be whole again, but you will never be the same. Nor should you be the same. Nor would you want to be the same.

Over time the absence of the loved one becomes less painful and more a normal part of your life. You do not forget. The memory of that person becomes embedded deeper and deeper into your heart and becomes a part of your continuing journey on this earth. All those little reminders come up through the course of your day. A particular association may occur one time a week, once a month, or intermittently. If we are open to opening our hearts, they can hold an infinite amount of love and caring, beyond what we can possibly imagine. We grieve indefinitely, and we cannot slough off our grief after some predetermined amount of time. The deaths of the ones we love and of others around us also bring a stark awareness of our own mortality.

Dealing with dying and death has many facets and intricacies. When your loved one is alive and suffering, you may wonder why this is happening to such a good person. When your loved one dies, you wonder what has happened to that person. Have they stopped suffering? Are they in a better place? Are they with the loved ones who have gone before them? There are so many unknown factors. That is where your faith comes in to assert that they are indeed in a better place. For myself, I have found that holding on to the memories of good times is helpful in remembering and honoring my loved ones.

Praying for all those souls of our loved ones keeps us connected with them. First, we pray that they will be resting in peace and have a place in heaven. I am not an expert in religion. I do not want them to wait to get to heaven bodily while their souls are already there. As stated, their bodies will be raised up at the end of time here on earth, and our hope is that they will be at peace. Secondly, I believe that they are the ones praying for us that those in this world will be well. It gives comfort to visualize our deceased loved ones hearing us in prayer.

Minute Meditation by Franciscan Media
FEBRUARY 13, 2017

Half the Battle

It is critical to the Christian life to accept the fact that whatever happens in your life is God's will. *It's* half the battle. The other half is learning to embrace suffering and uncomfortable situations as they arise.

—from *Faith, Hope & Clarity* by Gary Zimak

Is Grief a Form of Depression? *Detroit News* February 23, 2012, by Melissa Healy

Grief can be a long-lasting gut-wrenching never-seems-to-end frame of mind. The loss of a loved one can affect our whole disposition, concentration, and outlook on life. Is it the same as depression? In the Diagnostic and Statistical Manual's fifth edition, the editors of the British journal the Lancet have outlined in strong opposition to the new language, calling grief a natural and healthy response to loss, not a pathological state.

"Grief is not an illness. It is more usefully thought of as part of being human, and a normal response to the death of a loved one," writes the editor of the Lancet. "Most people who experience the death of someone they love do not need treatment by a psychiatrist or indeed by any doctor. For those who are grieving, doctors would do better to offer time, compassion, and empathy rather than a pill."

The current edition of the diagnostic manual states that if a patient's low mood and energy, sleep difficulties and appetite changes persist for more than two months following bereavement, a diagnosis of depression might be considered. That seems unrealistic. You cannot put a timetable on the amount of time a person grieves.

That theory of a two-month grieving process, if legitimate, would destroy my whole premise about death and grieving. I am strongly convinced that you must know yourself and let things take their course through the grieving process. Do what you need to do, not what someone tells you. I pray for those souls who have died, visit their resting place at the cemetery, and find reminders of them in different ways. For instance, my husband's mom loved birds and flowers. When I see birds perched on the window ledge for a brief second, we look at each other. It warms my heart, and I feel a bond with her. They also have a nest in every single tree around our home which is also a reminder.

In "Perspectives" published in Lancet, Harvard University medical anthropologist Arthur Kleinman agrees. He states, "Is grief something we can or should no longer tolerate?" Kleinman calls the current two-month time allowed for grief "a shockingly short expectation" that no religion or society would support.

Kleinman thinks this is sick. To allow grief to be redefined rewrites cultural values about how we understand and mark the loss of a fellow human being.

This theory does not state that all who grieve are depressed but says they should seek help for their suffering. Some say there is no difference between grief and depression. There are many characteristics that mimic each other, such as fatigue, feeling down, having a hard time concentrating, not finding any enjoyment in life, and being sad, to name a few of them.

Taking a pill to take away the pain of grieving only covers it up and does not make you feel like yourself. The Lancet's editor notes that there is no evidence that anti-depressant medications improve the moods of people who are healthy to begin with. Of course, the pharmaceutical manufacturers would be on board with the "depression" theory of grieving. "Its ubiquity makes grief a potential profit center for the business of psychiatry," writes Kleinman.

Minute Meditation by Franciscan Media
OCTOBER 1, 2014

Living in the Present

God extends his patience and generosity to us all. *It's* never too late to let go of past failures. We can always make a choice to do the right thing in the present moment. When we do God can bring it to good purpose.

—from *Fools, Liars, Cheaters, and Other Bible Heroes* by Barbara Hosbach

CHAPTER 8

Life Is Short: Other Stories

Unexpected Deaths

A friend, Kathy, from grade school and high school died at the young age of fifty-one. Kathy was extremely close with her mom, who had died a few years earlier. She never recovered from the loss. It was so sad. Kathy was a former military person who raised her two young children after getting a divorce, with the help of her parents. Even though she had a close relationship with her adult children, her mom was everything to her; it was too much, and she gave up living. I used to hang out at her parents' home when I was in grade school. I would ride my bike over to their house, and even if Kathy happened to be out would visit with her mom, who was a terrific lady. She welcomed me and everyone else.

My internal medicine doctor, who was an extremely caring person, died in a car accident, also at the age of fifty-one. I have not found another doctor who takes the time and cares as he did. This doctor did not just go through the motions, acting as though this were a production process. He looked at you, listened and talked *with* you, not *at* you. I have seen doctors who are talking and giving instructions as they are walking out the door. They do not have or take the time. Part of it is that they need to see so many patients for their practice to survive, which is understandable. As with so many things, there is a balance between patient care and the practice.

In a different instance, my dad's brother, Uncle Charlie, had rapidly declining health issues over a short period of time. Prior to that he had been active and, overall, healthy. He had diabetes but controlled it through food and exercise. He prided himself on checking his sugar religiously, altering his eating and adjusting his exercise as needed. If his sugar level happened to be high, he would go for a walk. That discipline was an example of fortitude and determination.

He was a huge family man and especially close with my dad, his brother. They were in business together and stayed close throughout their lives. After my dad passed, Uncle Charlie was devastated. Within months of my dad dying, Uncle Charlie began a downward spiral that started with a stroke. He had two of them in quick succession. He had to relearn reading and writing, along with sessions of speech and physical therapy. With the support and tremendous help from his family, he was able to gain back much of what he had lost.

Then he fell and had to go to the hospital. After a few days he stopped eating. He just refused. There were many family members trying to get him to eat, but to no avail. When I visited him two days before he died, I felt that he was letting go. After my uncle passed, the hospital did an autopsy at the family's request. They found he had a brain tumor. It is hard to imagine why they did not find this earlier, but they probably could not have improved his chances by that point. It was so sad. He was always upbeat and is greatly missed.

My husband's uncle and his dad's brother, Bob, passed away five days after being put on hospice care. Jim's dad went to visit him the day before he died. He spent the morning with him and the family, telling stories about growing up with him and their close friendship and respect for each other. Dad commented to me after Uncle Bob died that he was lying in the bed looking almost comatose, was not in pain, and seemed very peaceful. Different ailments have varying pain levels; hospice care and approach for treatment varies.

That really had him evaluating the hospice care his wife had received. That comparison also made me think of my dad. In both cases they were extremely uncomfortable and in pain. Although looking back is less than helpful, we acknowledge that we would have wanted these loved ones to be in less pain. Either we would have had to be more persistent in our requests, or the hospice could have provided guidelines that encouraged more pain medicine and more proactivity.

When I think about it, the period between my dad's getting on hospice and his death should have been considered extreme emergency. I think we could have made him more comfortable. My husband's dad said the same thing about his wife. He still feels bad years later that he could have given her more for her pain. How do we know when *later* is? How do we know the degree of their pain? In my dad's case, there was a mucous suction device that was set in the corner of the bedroom. My niece, who is a critical care nurse, and daughter used it to reduce some of the fluid that was building up. The average person without help from hospice would not have known of that need and may have thought this fluid buildup was normal.

We have many more relatives who are in poor health. There comes a time when our friends and relatives who came before us are all experiencing health issues and dying. The situation becomes tenuous, expecting to hear that the next person in this category finds out he has cancer, has broken bones after a fall, has some other serious health problem, or is no longer with us. Though based on a superstitious premise, it does many times seem to be the case that deaths come in threes.

A Day of Caring

I would rush to get to my parents' home on time, ideally early, to relieve the overnight person. There were the demands of having children in school, housekeeping, grocery shopping, paying bills, and volunteering as often as possible. When I got to their home, I would chat with the caregiver about how my mom and/or dad had been doing during the previous evening and overnight. I would put away the groceries and food I had prepared at home, check for any wash in the washer or dryer, start breakfast, read the notes from the night, refill the pill cases, call in any prescriptions, and anything else I could see that needed to be taken care of.

I would get frustrated with my dad because he could be spastic at times. He must have been lying low waiting for that person to leave. Shortly after the person left, I would start breakfast. During this time, I would get all his pills out to replenish his case. Within minutes I would hear his movement through the monitor. Thank goodness for that monitor, because, sure enough, he would be getting out of the bed.

He snored at times, and I got to know his breathing rhythm. He did not call out. I would say, "Dad, there is no reason to rush," but he still would. There was no holding him back. It was good he wanted to get up. He was incredible. Looking back, I think my dad was glad to see me, and I think I provided some comfort—or maybe that was wishful thinking. I would make him an omelet, bacon, and the toast he liked. Breakfast was big for him. I could tell he enjoyed his meal even though he was not overly expressive.

In my dad's case, if we had not constantly pushed and encouraged him, he would have had little quality of life. He would have sat or lain in bed without hope. Although it was difficult at times, he could get up out of bed, walk to the bathroom, brush his teeth—sometimes, eat, watch tv, listen to music, and carry out many other day-to-day activities, even if in a limited way. It was different every day. If we did not try each day, he would have regressed.

There were times he could not walk, and we had to push him in his walker chair. Sometimes, by the afternoon my dad was back to moving again. If we had conveyed to him a cannot-do instead of can-do attitude, he would not have continued to function and move. He would, I am convinced, have died years earlier. It was that pushing and encouragement that kept him going. We were there with him every minute. He had a lot of love and support. We gave my dad some purpose, in small ways, to keep going. A little love and encouragement go a long way.

It was the same with my mom. She enjoyed having people around. All her family gave her a lot of positive support, and, unlike the situation with my dad, we could talk about current and past events. Although my dad did not talk much, he still did listen. Together they were both a force and a remarkable example. Their roles as parents, and in later years as friends, propelled us to help them; their example of trying to do the best they could each day set a great example.

It is not always possible to get the one-on-one care my mom and dad were able to have. In my parents' case, they remained in their own home with up to eight outside caregivers whom I hired, trained, and paid; unfortunately, I also had to fire a few. They became a part of their lives. The alternatives for the aging parent are to live at one of the children's homes or in an assisted living or nursing home. It would be rare to get one-on-one attention constantly in nursing or assisted living facilities. There are so many assisted living and nursing care facilities where the residents or patients are sitting in wheelchairs or in bed all day, without any activity or stimulation. Realistically, the ratio of staff to residents or patients does not allow the attention each person would need, especially not in terms of a one-on-one scenario.

My uncle lived in an assisted living facility, which worked well for him. I was constantly in touch with the nurse and staff there. If not visiting, I would call at various times to check on how he was doing. As he had increasing limitations and health issues, his medications changed, he required additional doctor appointments, he needed his blood checked daily, and it was necessary on a regular basis to make sure he was clean.

Taking care of someone requires the highest form of unconditional love. There are no bells, whistles, cheers, or "Great job!" accolades. It is the inner desire to do the right thing and your inner satisfaction that push you to go on. I do not want to look back and say I should have done this or that. In all honesty, part of those feelings stems from my upbringing of feeling perpetually guilty—but guilt, despite its obvious downsides, is still a good motivator.

It is not about what other people see but about what we know inside ourselves. We will answer to a higher being. What we put into life determines what we get out of life. If we allow it to happen, we will learn from all the struggles and sorrows that come our way. The hope is that we will indeed have the willingness to accept the things we cannot change, the courage to change the things we can, and the wisdom to know the difference.

Minute Meditation by Franciscan Media
JANUARY 29, 2017

Open the Door

We face so many challenges in life: poverty, distress, humiliation, the struggle for justice, persecutions, and many others. But if we open the door to Jesus and allow him to be part of our lives, if we share our joys and sorrows with him, then we will experience the peace and joy that only God, who is infinite love, can give.

—from *The Spirit of Saint Francis*

CHAPTER 9

Discoveries Made: The Big and Easy, Maintaining a Positive Attitude

A S CAREGIVERS, WE encourage and sometimes push those we are caring for through the day. If we did not do this, our loved one would in many cases not have a reason to exist. It is the pushing, encouraging, and coaxing to have them do something that ignites their desire. It not only gives them a reason to exist but imparts meaning in their life.

Exercise and drinking water are two of the important necessities that are *big* (exercise) and *easy* (drinking water). Everyone needs to be hydrated. Dehydration can be a problem for all ages, but especially the elderly. It requires a conscious effort to drink water, even if one does not like it. Dehydration is a concern and common problem with the elderly, especially if that person lives alone, may not always be cognizant of the importance of hydration throughout the day, or simply does not drink water.

It sounds easy: drink water to hydrate. In my mom's case, she did not like to drink water. When she went through the motions of drinking, it looked as though the water reproduced and made more in the glass! Coffee was different; she had no problem drinking that because she liked it. In my dad's case, he fortunately did drink a good amount of water daily; his constipation was a major issue that was exacerbated by the Parkinson's. Water is critical for everyone's system. It helps with going to the bathroom, avoiding urinary tract infections (UTIs), and preventing dehydration. Pop, coffee, and other flavored drinks do not help the system in the way water does. For my mom, this required constant reminders and nudging; with 24/7 care she always had a coach around her.

Making It Better and Doing the Right Thing

At times, instead of taking actions to do the right thing, we get so desperate to make things better that we go to extreme extents. We do not see clearly. Sometimes we get so focused on getting that person better that we lose focus on what is best for them. When do we know we have pushed far enough? What is meant by comfort measures? Is it okay to let the person sit and do nothing?

The truth is, in many cases the person is not going to get better. How do we know? We observe; follow their medical developments; talk with the doctors; and make an intelligent, common-sense determination. I talked with the medical doctors, therapists, caregivers, and all who were involved with each person's care to get a comprehensive picture of what was going on with them. There were in some cases the possibility and hope that they would get better. But emotions can cloud your perception of a situation and hinder your decision-making ability. The other fact is that we do not have control over many things in life. Although it is not easy to do, taking the position to control what we can and accept what we cannot is always the right, though difficult, approach.

A doctor does not generally know what is wrong by just looking at you or the person you are caring for. You, the caregiver, need to explain, to give them information and a description of the symptoms. In the case of taking care of someone who cannot communicate clearly, as a caregiver you need to understand the patient. This requires being an active participant in their life: knowing what their everyday activities encompass, observing how they are currently, looking at their medications, and knowing what they are taking them for. Ask questions. Are there any counterreactions with other medications, and what might be the side effects? Have they become more agitated? Do they have a rash? Are they going to the bathroom regularly? Is their urine dark? Are they dehydrated from not drinking enough water? Does their blood work show anything off balance?

It is the medical advocate who makes the decisions if the patient or caregiver is incapable of providing answers. If that patient must see a doctor, go to the hospital, or have a test or procedure done, they need a medical advocate who can speak for them. It is helpful if your loved one can make their wishes known before getting to this point. When the time comes, this will lessen family disagreements about the course of care for the patient.

My uncle was in and out of the hospital. I was asked too many times to count by the doctors if they should resuscitate him if needed. I needed to sign a DNR (Do Not Resuscitate) form with the doctors and hospital each time, even though we continually went to the same hospital. The copy of the form had to be posted at the assisted living facility my uncle was at. It is good to know your loved one's wishes and be ready to answer some of the life-and-death questions that could arise.

Who Is home Today?

Our loved ones' mental and physical health can fluctuate regularly. We do not know how they will act and feel from day to day. Things can be up one minute and down the next. Your loved one could be flying high one day and low the next. It may be a chore for them to get up and get through the day. This fluctuation applies as well to the caregiver who is riding this rollercoaster with the highs and lows. Anyone who is caring for someone with dementia and Alzheimer's disease knows that they can seem perfectly normal one minute and the next become agitated, aggressive, or lost and in another world.

Treatment of the Elderly

If your loved one has advanced dementia or Alzheimer's, you could rationalize that they do not know what is going on and question whether it matters what you say or do. However, depending on the extent of their dementia, there may be times when they are lucid and comprehending. No doubt they can still feel. The dementia can make them act like a child, and the biggest challenge is that they be secure and have boundaries, like a child. The difference is that the premise of doing things the right way goes out the window. Who are we to say they cannot do something?

For instance, at a young age we are shown how to use utensils. Then, due to physical and mental limitations, some patients can no longer use them as an adult. This is an adjustment for them and you. For instance, the dignified norm for eating in our culture is to use utensils, not one's fingers. It is easier to help a toddler learn to use utensils than to coach an adult with limitations. The person's ability to use motor skills, like grasping and holding a utensil, is critical. To really know that person and their ability level requires being with them, observing, interacting, and listening.

If an activity is not physically hurting them, then why not encourage them to engage in it? Some days it may not be possible, and this is alright. In my dad's case, he could use the utensils sometimes and on other times resorted to using his fingers. The irony is that this person instilled in me early on the importance of using utensils. The patient may have been the very one who enforced these rules, encouraged, taught, and worked for your wellbeing, and now you are doing that for them. The roles have been reversed.

Attitude

The attitude of all involved makes a difference. It is all about the approach. There are times we are overwhelmed by the task at hand. There seems to be no light at the end of the tunnel. You know the person is not doing well and, in many cases, is in fact dying. There is no choice but to take one day at a time. We talk about how the attitude of the person suffering affects their situation, but how about our attitude? That person is relying on us. What is our persona? Do we go into their home as though this is a burden or a drag, or do we convey honestly that we are happy to see them? They can feel and sense love throughout their journey, and at the end it is not *what* we do but *how* we do it.

Attitude does play a huge role in how each person handles their ailment and life's challenges. It takes effort every day to push yourself, get up each morning, get dressed, exercise, eat well, reach out to another person, and find meaning as to why you are here on this earth. It makes a huge difference that your loved one knows they are not alone. They have their faith in God and rely on the people here on earth.

There is a difference between people who grab ahold of life and those who let it slip away. Yes, we all have bad times. Change is hard. It can be harder for some people than for others. Do we accept our fate and ultimate destiny? Or do we deny that something is wrong and retreat into a shell? Life entails so many unknowns. It helps so much if we are accepting and somewhat adaptable to change. A wholehearted positive approach to life and mindfulness instills the attitude through which we find our meaning.

Helping with ADLs

There are many functions with which we can assist during the day; among others, these may include showering; bathing; putting in eye drops; administering medicine; or going to the doctor, dentist, or therapist. It is natural to resent the time and energy outlay the person requires from you. Then there is the guilt over feeling resentful. It becomes a struggle. As more demands are placed on you, the struggle becomes greater, both mentally and physically.

My dad did better by moving as much as he could. His quality of life was better at each stage because we kept him active. Like most things in life, there is a risk/reward factor. The risk was that he could fall and get hurt, choke by eating by himself, or risk a slew of other negative outcomes. If we fed him, we would control how much he put into his mouth. However, if he could still eat on his own, why would we deny him this function? Yes, it was a messy, risky business, but it gave him a sense of independence, which was critical. A constant weighing in on whether to do things the easy or the hard way takes diligence.

Physically Assisting

There are right ways and wrong ways to physically help someone. For instance, they should not be pulled up by their arms. That puts too much stress on their shoulders; if pulled too hard, their arms could come out of their sockets. It would not take much to do this with someone who is frail. The limitations of the person you are caring for factor in, but having them do as much as possible to help themselves is physiologically better for them.

Gardening to Feel Good

Working in the dirt is therapeutic. Not everyone may agree with this. However, it is going back to basics that helps keep a person rooted. There is something about breathing the air, looking up at the sky, seeing the sunshine, and working outside that give a sense of inner peace and keep an individual stable. Gardening makes many people happy. Gardening can help to ease and heal both the mind and the body.

> *Researchers found that a common microbe in soil, Mycobacterium vaccae, triggers the release of serotonin in the brain.* Serotonin is the body's natural anti-depressant that keeps us happy *and also* strengthens the immune system. A simple way to activate this microbe is by weeding. The microbe is inhaled. Gardeners inhale these microscopic bacteria when moving soil around. Even without weeding, a puff of dust is elevated by a gust of wind. So, just getting out in the green space and breathing in the fresh air can do wonders for your spirits. (Nancy Szerlag, *The Detroit News*, July 15, 2018)

The manual labor we do in the flower beds and garden is physical and can be richly satisfying. When we experience visible results from the earth, we find solace and peace in an otherwise fragmented world. On the other hand, gardens teach us disappointment when bugs or four-legged critters destroy our hard effort, or the once beautiful flowers and plants die. Growing something, anything, is a lesson in patience and love. Gardens fill us with gratitude. With this said, gardening is not for everyone. Not everyone has the time, energy, or desire to work in the dirt. The point is to find your own inner equilibrium in some satisfying venture.

I equate weeding with embracing what life dishes out. Weeding is probably one of the most menial tasks to undertake, but it can be therapeutic. The dirt and earth are our foundation. Do you cover up the weeds with dirt, just pull the surface growth, or dig in to get the root? If you pull only the tops of the weeds, they will stay that way for a short time but will come back. By pulling up the root you get down to the nitty gritty, their source.

To be humble, to accept our limits, is to find our grounding in becoming fulfilled. When we strive against those limits, our situation becomes unbearable. And we become miserable. Like the soil that erodes, we become dissatisfied with our life. It is good to strive to do more and be better, but knowing who we are gives us a boundary to gauge ourselves. It is a fine line to do and strive for more, while at the same time maintaining balance.

Changing your routine keeps things moving; you feel fresh and alert. This can help you to adjust your way of thinking and acting toward a loved one. Instead of going through the motions and doing what is required throughout the day, you must think about what you are doing. This can help you gain a new perspective. Is this only a surface relationship? "Hi, I am here for a visit, and in a short time I will be gone." Or do you really find out what is going on? Do you ask questions? Do you really try to see that person at this moment in time, not the way they were in the past?

Minute Meditation by Franciscan Media
OCTOBER 24, 2019

Our Physical Surroundings Are Holy

We who tend to think of nature as nothing more than a usable commodity can learn a great deal from Francis's relationship with the environment. He teaches us the liberating truth that our physical surroundings are holy only because they *aren't* purely physical. Instead, *they're* permeated through and through with the Spirit and beauty of God. In a mysterious way that the mind *can't* fathom but the heart knows full well, we don't just dwell in God's world. In dwelling in God's world, we also abide in God himself.

—from the book *The Humility of God: a Franciscan Perspective* by Ilia Delio, OSF

CHAPTER 10

My Story

S UFFERING MENTALLY, EMOTIONALLY, and physically is a part of life. It is hard to stay upbeat and positive when day in and day out you must struggle through everything you do. When caring for someone, the question becomes whether this person really must suffer through so much. For you as a caregiver, it may seem as though your efforts are not enough. However, what you put into caring correlates with how much you get out of it. Are you vested, or is this just something you should do, an obligation? This issue has required me to challenge my own thinking and habits. Many times, I must acknowledge that I am struggling and lost. After this happens, however, you will be found. God's committed presence gives us hope.

It is hard to imagine what someone else is going through. It has been years since my dad died. I have said many times to myself how thankful I am that I can use all my limbs to be able to help myself. It is extremely difficult to care for someone who is barely able to function at the most basic capacity. The one thing I have always appreciated most is the ability to physically function, be flexible, move, and engage in activities. That has drastically changed for me. For at least two years I had lower back pain and discomfort that I could work through by stretching. Although I was not as limber as I once was, I could function. This was during a terribly busy time with taking care of my dad and our own household.

Assisting my dad became more and more physically demanding. Most times I needed to physically help him. He could not always get up on his own from the bed or chair. A specific repetitive action I did that exacerbated my problem was to help my dad get in and out of his shower; he took one every day. I used my foot to push his foot up and over the sill, while holding his upper body steady so he could hold the grab bars to get into the shower and to the chair to sit. The entry to the shower stall was extremely narrow, making it a challenge for my dad and whomever was helping him. With Parkinson's, his body was rigid, and his brain could not register the need to lift his foot. That action of my using my foot to push his foot up without bending aggravated my back issues. Why go through all that? The shower relaxed him. He wanted his body to feel clean, it relieved tension, and I could tell how much he liked it. It gave him a boost for tackling the day. The reward was far greater than the risk.

You do not realize until something incapacitating happens to you how bad it is. The winter of 2017 really did me in. I do not want to talk about myself, but this aspect is part of caregiving. Your needs are overshadowed by the needs of the person you are caring for. Physically and mentally, everything eventually catches up with you. In my case, the thing that caught up with me was sciatica. It was literally a pain in the ass/butt! The sciatica was attributed to a bulging disc from straining my muscles over a long period of time. It went from my lower left side of my back into my butt/piriformis, skipping the thigh, down the calf and into my ankle.

The pain was excruciating and debilitating. It was barely possible to carry out basic movements. My limbs just would not cooperate and work, and my pace went from fast to slow to slower. This lasted intensely for almost a year, until gradually, with physical therapy and time, it got better. That was something I had not experienced before. I am grateful I have gotten back to being able to function. I get some discomfort, pain, and stiffness, but am so glad to be able to operate.

I have gone most of my life thinking I could plow through, charge ahead, and push myself, assuring myself that everything is about mind over matter, reasoning that I could control my mind and body. Ha! Think again. That is not the case with sciatica. Readers who have or have had this fully understand what I mean. My experience helped put into perspective how challenging and exhausting life can be with limitations. People with long-term illness struggle every day. It is understandable for them to say they cannot go on and want to give up.

The physical therapist told me not to engage in any activity that would trigger the pain. This was the first time I was stopped in my tracks. I could not force myself to physically get things done as I usually did. It is difficult to imagine what another person may be going through. It is easy to convince yourself that you can overcome this or that. Some common internal directives are to have a positive attitude, refrain from being depressed, and charge ahead through those handicaps!

When the person you are caring for is struggling to breathe, move, eat, drink, go to the bathroom, hear, see, and all the things we so easily do, that advice is easier said than done. That person is probably thinking these expectations are nuts! *I cannot do that. Leave me alone.* Even though it is difficult, positive, proactive encouragement really does make a difference and shows that you care, even though you cannot totally change the circumstances.

There are two thought patterns when you are going through a debilitating medical condition. You can either stay stagnant with fear or plow ahead. In my instance, the sciatica created anxiety that caused inaction on my part. I was afraid to put pressure or weight on my ankle. There was a fifty-percent fear factor that stopped me. It was the fear that if I did something it would trigger that pain. One can become frozen to inaction by their fears. I have learned more about other people through my own struggles.

This development led me to becoming a "mall walker," as we call ourselves. Over the years for one reason or another I have gone to the mall early in the morning to walk. The mall used to allow us entry at about 6:00 a.m. when the security guard would open a door. I tried getting in before that time, but, unfortunately, that did not last, and I was told I could not be inside yet. Then they started opening the doors at 8:00 a.m. Sometimes you could enter a little earlier. When my youngest son was a baby until he was about two years old, I would push him in his stroller. He was very social. He would hang over the stroller, wave, and talk to everyone as I was passing them by. They wanted me to stop; instead, I would simply say "hi" as I sped by.

I am not just talking about walkers but *mall walkers*. This is a world all its own. It is amazing how many people are aging and struggling. Some can barely walk. When I had the sciatica, I was in the barely walking category! I have seen so many elderly and younger people making those laps through the mall. There are people with walkers, canes, hunched over, hugging the wall, and so much more. They are sometimes in a group, sometimes walking four abreast, which blocks the runway. It gets annoying. That makes it tough to maneuver if you are going at a good clip. Some are moving slowly and some faster. There are all types of people who walk and use it as an opportunity to socialize with their peers.

These are the courageous ones who put themselves out there. Some cannot drive but find a way to get to the mall. They may be going as slowly as molasses, but they are going. Instead of staying at home, they put themselves out there. Every time you go, you see the same groups walking and talking. They may be discussing their own personal struggles, politics, or any number of other topics. It would be easier to stay at home and not get out, which makes this effort amazing and inspiring. These people, the mall walkers, are talking with each other, walking to the best of their ability, smiling, and laughing. They keep track and care about each other's well-being. They walk their walk, talk their talk, buy a coffee, discuss whatever is on their minds. It is the best form of therapy. They get encouragement from the other walkers and have built up comradery with them. It is a community. I recently saw some of the same people I did when I would take my son in his stroller when he was a few years old. He is now in his twenties!

Going through that period of my own problems really enlightened me as to how difficult it is for some of these individuals to stay positive. You keep working through the obstacles and hopefully eventually will get better. For those who have an illness or disease that they know is not going to improve, special strength is needed, both by that person and their caregiver. It is an inner strength that keeps them going.

Minute Meditation by Franciscan Media
JUNE 25, 2020

Faith Is the Opposite of Anxiety

For Jesus, faith is not opposed to not believing in God; it *doesn't* mean you go to church, or that you're into religion or that you say "Lord, Lord!" (*see* Matthew 7:21). Faith for Jesus is the opposite of anxiety. If you are anxious, if you are trying to control everything, if you are worried about many things, you *don't* have faith, according to Jesus. You do not trust that God is Good and on your side. *You're* trying to do it all yourself, lift yourself up by your own bootstraps. The giveaway is control. *That's* a good litmus test of the quality of your faith. People of faith *don't* have to control everything, nor do they have to change people. You have the wisdom to know the difference, as the Twelve-Step people say. You cannot "fix" the soul. "Set your hearts on this kingdom first, and on God's saving justice, and all these other things will be given you as well. So do not worry about tomorrow: tomorrow will take care of itself" (Matthew 6:33–34a).

—from *Jesus' Plan for a New World: The Sermon on the Mount*

CHAPTER 11

Faith, Hope, Love, and Prayers: Moving Forward on the Journey

Minute Meditation by Franciscan Media
OCTOBER 5, 2019

We Are Called to Follow

Francis followed in the footsteps of Jesus, and that is where most of us falter. We want to follow Jesus's footsteps but know ahead of time where they lead, and we are afraid. We hold back. In his writings Francis never used the word *imitate* in relation to Christ; instead, he used the phrase "to follow in the footsteps of Christ." Christ's invitation was to "follow me" (Matthew 10:38), not "imitate me." In following Christ, the self that one thinks has been lost is found, so that as one walks in the footsteps of Christ a whole and realized true self begins to emerge.

—from the book *Mystics: Twelve Who Reveal God's Love* by Murray Bodo, OFM

Seek and You Shall Find

Not everyone is able to care for a loved one. You may think *I am only one person; what can I do?* The answer is plenty! We all have some path to follow, whether or not we know what that path may be. With the help of God, we can do more than our mind could ever hope for or imagine. Each one of us is unique and has special abilities, with all that is good inside of us being utilized to help our loved one and others.

Throughout our lives we need something to sustain us, along with our gift of living here on earth. Prayer and the closeness with God can help us maneuver through all life's obstacles. Along with this inner coexistence, it is important to have support and help. This is coming from someone who is pretty much a loner and tries to do everything myself. My husband has been my rock, safeguard, and amour through all these years. I would be one of the last people to admit this, but we all need people.

Life is a journey. The journey is in the little steps we take. One of the greatest outcomes of caring for my parents and uncle was that our children and all the nieces and nephews bonded with them. They were active participants in caring for them. My youngest son consistently came with me to visit my uncle at the assisted living facility, hospital, and rehab. Early on, he had an incredibly special bond that has remained with him to this day. My other children helped with my parents, whether it was to pick them up to come over for dinner or stay with them to fill in for someone. My nieces and nephews did the same thing. They would go out with them shopping, eat with them at a restaurant, and help with their daily activities. They hung out with them when coming home from college and when they lived in another state. This is the legacy we want; I am grateful my children and family have this priceless heritage.

The process of aging and declining health is daunting for the person, those caring for them, and all their loved ones. It is uncanny after your loved one dies how you get reminders of them through other people and activities you undertake. Gratefulness breeds an inner strength that propagates peace and joy in our lives. The journey of life, with all its ups, downs, obstacles, and struggles, is the reward.

From gratefulness comes *grace*, which is the inner self extending to our outer being. I try to live with this motto each day: Greet each day with purpose. Respect everyone. Accept what is here before you today, not what was or what you think will be. Care for all you encounter. Embrace life.

Acknowledgments

You want to help. You are pulled in many directions. It helps to have good support. It helps to have outside interests. It helps to exercise. It helps to pray. It helps to have family. It helps to have positive social interactions, family, and friends. Anything to maintain some semblance of order and balance in your hectic life. For me, my husband is my best friend, confidant, and stabilizer.

I am thankful for my husband, who has been on this journey with me; my children, who have inspired me; my sisters and brothers, nieces and nephews, friends and extended family who are always positive and helpful.

Minute Meditation by Franciscan Media
JULY 17, 2017

God Is the Only True Happiness

Unless I am connected to God, who invented the happiness I'm seeking, I come up frustrated, angry, and disappointed by life—empty instead of full. When I feel disconnected from God, I feel restless—not at peace with myself, with my God, or with others.
—from the book *Born to Soar: Unleashing God's Word in Your Life*

Made in the USA
Middletown, DE
23 September 2022

10925168R00060